797,885 Books
are available to read at

www.ForgottenBooks.com

Forgotten Books' App
Available for mobile, tablet & eReader

ISBN 978-1-330-57493-5
PIBN 10080713

This book is a reproduction of an important historical work. Forgotten Books uses state-of-the-art technology to digitally reconstruct the work, preserving the original format whilst repairing imperfections present in the aged copy. In rare cases, an imperfection in the original, such as a blemish or missing page, may be replicated in our edition. We do, however, repair the vast majority of imperfections successfully; any imperfections that remain are intentionally left to preserve the state of such historical works.

Forgotten Books is a registered trademark of FB &c Ltd.
Copyright © 2015 FB &c Ltd.
FB &c Ltd, Dalton House, 60 Windsor Avenue, London, SW19 2RR.
Company number 08720141. Registered in England and Wales.

For support please visit www.forgottenbooks.com

1 MONTH OF FREE READING

at

www.ForgottenBooks.com

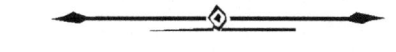

By purchasing this book you are eligible for one month membership to ForgottenBooks.com, giving you unlimited access to our entire collection of over 700,000 titles via our web site and mobile apps.

To claim your free month visit:

www.forgottenbooks.com/free80713

* Offer is valid for 45 days from date of purchase. Terms and conditions apply.

Similar Books Are Available from
www.forgottenbooks.com

Sacred Songs and Solos
Twelve Hundred Hymns, by Ira David Sankey

David
Shepherd, Psalmist, King, by F. B. Meyer

The Christian Hymnal
Hymns With Tunes for the Services of the Church, by Frank Sewell

A Complete Concordance to the Holy Scriptures
by John Eadie

Blossoms from a Believer's Garden
by Frances Ridley Havergal

A Book of Prayer
From the Public Ministrations of Henry Ward Beecher, by Henry Ward Beecher

The Chief Sufferings of Life, and Their Remedies
by Abbe Ephrem Duhaut

Companions of the Sorrowful Way
by John Watson

The Complete Works of Stephen Charnock, Vol. 1
by Stephen Charnock

Hymns from the Rigveda
Selected and Metrically Translated, by A. A. Macdonell

Counsel and Comfort for Daily Life
by Unknown Author

Hymn and Tune Book, for the Church and the Home
by American Unitarian Association

Meditations on the Sacred Passion of Our Lord
by Cardinal Wiseman

Devotions Upon Emergent Occasions
Together With Death's Duel, by John Donne

The Divine Processional
by Denis Wortman

Evening Thoughts
by Frances Ridley Havergal

The Every Day of Life
by James Russell Miller

Family Prayers
by Lyman P. Powell

Church Psalmist, or Psalms and Hymns
For the Public, Social, and Private Use of Evangelical Christians, by Free Will Baptists

Guide to Non-Liturgical Prayer
For Clergymen and Laymen, by John C. Clyde

THE
WESLEYAN PSALMIST

OR

SONGS OF CANAAN,

A COLLECTION OF

HYMNS AND TUNES

DESIGNED TO BE USED AT CAMP-MEETINGS, AND AT CLASS AND PRAYER MEETINGS, AND OTHER OCCASIONS OF SOCIAL DEVOTION.

COMPILED BY M. L. SCUDDER,

OF THE NEW-ENGLAND CONFERENCE.

Speaking to yourselves in Psalms and Hymns and spiritual songs, singing and making melody in your hearts to the Lord.—PAUL.

BOSTON:
D. S. KING, NO. 1 CORNHILL.
LOWELL: E. A. RICE.   PHILADELPHIA: J. HARMSTEAD.

1842.

Entered according to Act of Congress, in the year 1842,
By M. L. SCUDDER,
In the Clerk's Office of the District Court for the District of Massachusetts.

STEREOTYPED BY KIDDER AND WRIGHT, BOSTON.

INTRODUCTION.

No further apology can be necessary for issuing this edition of the "*Wesleyan Psalmist*" enlarged and much improved from its precedent, the *Songs of Canaan*, than to say that all of a very large edition of the latter work have already been sold, and orders are frequently received for more. It is but proper to state that this work although in one sense a second edition will be found to have many claims beyond the former— 1st. Many new tunes of great popularity are introduced. 2. Although the price is nearly the same, it will contain about twice the number of tunes and more than twice the number of hymns. 3. It will be printed on much better paper, and much better executed. 4. Owing to the haste in which the former edition passed the press, many errors escaped uncorrected; it is believed that this will be a more correct edition. And 5th. Great pains have been taken in the selection of *several* appropriate Hymns to most of the tunes so as to render it a proper supplement to the regular Hymn book both in the class and Prayer meeting. It has been thought best by those concerned to fix the price of this work so low that all who wish may readily be able to supply themselves.

It might not be anticipated that such a work as this would be found beyond strict criticism, yet it is hoped that as little occasion for this is given as in the nature of the case could be expected.

The compiler feels indebted to Mr. *J. B. Packard* for the considerable aid he has afforded him in harmonizing and arranging many of the tunes in this little book; also to several of the members of the *Providence*, *New England* and *New Hampshi*re Conferences for their willing and efficient services— may we sing with the Spirit and with the Understanding also.

THE COMPILER.

BOSTON SEPT. 26. 1842.

THE
WESLEYAN PSALMIST.

REMEMBER ME. C. M.
Arranged and Harmonized for this work.

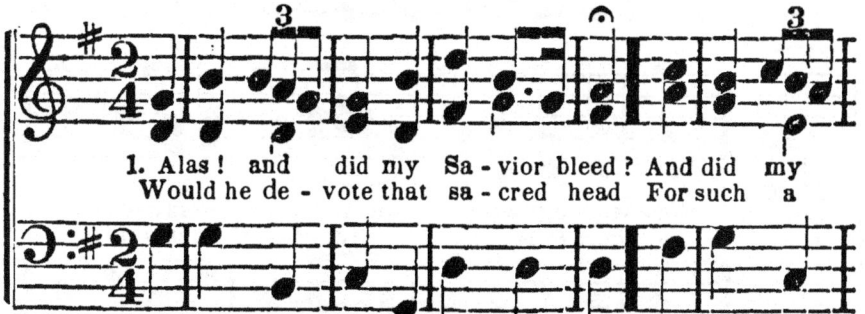

1. Alas! and did my Sa-vior bleed? And did my
Would he de-vote that sa-cred head For such a

Re-mem-ber me, Re-mem-ber me, Dear Lord, re-
Re-mem-ber, Lord, thy dy-ing groans, And then re-

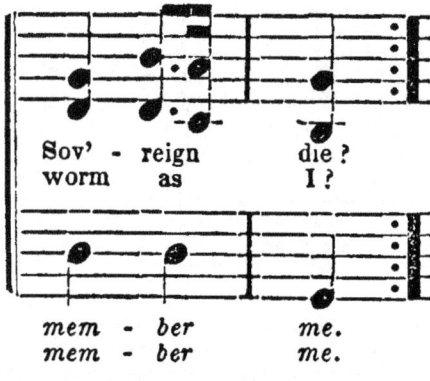

Sov'-reign die?
worm as I?

mem - ber me.
mem - ber me.

2 Was it for crimes that I have done,
He groan'd upon the tree?
Amazing pity! grace unknown!
And love beyond degree!

3 Well might the sun in darkness hide,
And shut his glories in;
When Christ the mighty Maker died,
For man the creature's sin.
Remember me, &c.

4 Thus might I hide my blushing face,
While his dear cross appears;
Dissolve my heart in thankfulness
And melt mine eyes to tears.
Remember me, &c.

5 But drops of grief can ne'er repay
The debt of love I owe;
Here, Lord, I give myself away,
'Tis all that I can do.
Remember me, &c.

NOTE.—*During the great revival at Bennett Street, Boston, in 1842, this tune was an especial favorite.*

4. O! that will be joyful. C. M.

Arranged for this work.

NOTE.—Perhaps no tune has been more extensively used than this during the past year—1842.

joy - ful, Oh that will be joy - ful to meet to part no more.

2 Should earth against my soul en-
    gage,
And fiery darts be hurl'd,
Then I can smile at Satan's rage,
    And face a frowning world.
    Oh that will be joyful, &c.

3 Let cares like a wild deluge come,
    Let storms of sorrow fall;
So I but safely reach my home,
    My God, my heaven, my all:
    Oh that will be joyful, &c.

4 There I shall bathe my weary soul,
    In seas of heavenly rest,
And not a wave of trouble roll
    Across my peaceful breast.
    Oh that will be joyful, &c.

5 The saints in all this glorious war,
    Shall conquer, though they die;
They see the triumph from afar,
    By faith they bring it nigh.
    Oh that will be joyful, &c.

6 When that illustrious day shall rise
    And all thy armies shine
In robes of victory through the skies,
    The glory shall be thine.
    Oh that will be joyful, &c.

7 When we've been there ten thousand years,
    Bright shining as the sun;
We've no less days to sing God's praise,
    Than when we first begun.
    Oh that will be joyful, &c.

Christian Union.

1 Our souls by love together knit,
    Cemented, mix'd in one,
One hope, one heart, one mind, one voice,
    'Tis heav'n on earth begun.
    Oh that will be joyful, &c.

2 Our hearts have often burn'd within,
    And glow'd with sacred fire,
While Jesus spoke, and fed, and blest,
    And fill'd th' enlarg'd desire.
    Oh that will be joyful, &c.

3 And when thou mak'st thy jewels up,
    And set'st thy starry crown;
When all thy sparkling gems shall shine,
    Proclaim'd by thee thine own.
    Oh that will be joyful, &c.

4 May we, a little band of love,
    We sinners, sav'd by grace,
From glory unto glory chang'd,
    Behold thee face to face.
    Oh that will be joyful, &c.

5 Together let us sweetly live,
    Together let us die;
And each a starry crown receive,
    And reign above the sky.
    Oh that will be joyful, &c.

6 Then when the mighty work is wrought,
    Receive thy ready bride;
Give us in heaven a happy lot,
    With all the sanctified.
    Oh that will be joyful, &c.

CORONATION. C. M. — O. HOLDEN.

NOTE.—*This tune is at once recognized as the old favorite of every lover of devotional singing.*

1. All hail the great Immanuel's name, Let angels prostrate fall; Bring forth the royal di-a-dem, And crown him Lord of all— Bring forth the royal di-a-dem, And crown him Lord of all.

2
Crown him, ye morning stars of light,
Who fix'd this floating ball; (might
Now hail the strength of Israel's
And crown him—Lord of all.

3
Crown him, ye martyrs of our God,
Who from his altar call;
Extol the stem of Jesse's rod,
And crown him—Lord of all.

4
Ye chosen seed of Israel's race,
Ye ransom'd from the fall;
Hail him who saves you by his grace,
And crown him—Lord of all.

5
Sinners, whose love can ne'er forget
The wormwood and the gall,
Go spread your trophies at his feet,
And crown him—Lord of all.

WESLEYAN PSALMIST.

The Heavenly Canaan.

1 On Jordan's stormy banks I stand,
  And cast a wishful eye,
To Canaan's fair and happy land,
  Where my possessions lie.

2 O the transporting, rapt'rous scene,
  That rises to my sight !
Sweet fields array'd in living green,
  And rivers of delight !

3 All o'er those wide extended plains,
  Shines one eternal day ;
There God the Son forever reigns
  And scatters night away.

4 No chilling winds, nor pois'nous (breath,
  Can reach that healthful shore ;
Sickness and sorrow, pain and death,
  Are felt and fear'd no more.

5 When shall I reach that happy
  And be forever blest ; (place,
When shall I see my Father's face,
  And in his bosom rest ?

6 Fill'd with delight, my raptur'd
  Would here no longer stay ! (soul
Though Jordan's waves around me (roll,
  Fearless I'd launch away.

The Gospel Message.

1 O for a thousand tongues to sing
  My great Redeemer's praise !
The glories of my God and King,
  The triumphs of his grace !

2 My gracious Master, and my God,
  Assist me to proclaim,
To spread through all the earth a-
  The honors of thy Name. (broad

3 Jesus !—the Name that charms our (fears,
  That bids our sorrows cease ;
'Tis music in the sinner's ears,
  'Tis life, and health, and peace.

4 He breaks the power of cancell'd
  He sets the prisoner free ; (sin,
His blood can make the foulest clean,
  His blood avail'd for *me*.

5 He speaks, and listening to his
  New life the dead receive ; (voice
The mournful, broken hearts rejoice,
  The humble poor believe.

6 Hear him, ye deaf ; his praise, ye (dumb,
  Your loosen'd tongues employ ;
Ye blind, behold your Savior come,
  And leap, ye lame, for joy.

THE BLEEDING SAVIOR. C. M.

1. A - las ! and did my Savior bleed ? And did my Sov'reign die?
The Lamb, the Lamb, the loving Lamb, The Lamb on Calvary ;

Would he devote his sacred head For such a worm as I ?
The Lamb was slain, but lives again, To in-ter-cede for me.

2 Was it for crimes that I have done,
  He groaned upon the tree ;
Amazing pity ! grace unknown !
  And love beyond degree !
    The Lamb, &c.

3 Well might the sun in darkness
  And shut his glories in ; (hide,
When Christ, the mighty Maker died,
  For man the creature's sin !
    The Lamb, &c.

4 Thus might I hide my blushing face,
  When his dear cross appears ;
Dissolve my heart in thankfulness,
  And melt mine eyes to tears.
    The Lamb, &c.

5 But drops of grief can ne'er repay
  The debt of love I owe ;
Here, Lord, I give myself away,
  'Tis all that I can do.
    The Lamb, &c.

8 THE PRODIGAL'S RETURN. C. M.

Arranged for this work.

NOTE.—*This is a proper Hymn and tune to be sung on the return of Backsliders.*

1. Afflictions though they seem severe, In mercy oft are sent, They stopp'd the prodigal's career And caused him to re-pent. I'll die no more for bread, I'll die no more for bread, he cried, Nor starve [in foreign lands, My father's house hath large supplies, And bounteous are his [hands.

2 What have I gained by sin, he said,
   But hunger, shame and fear;
My father's house abounds with bread,
   While I am starving here.
      I'll die no more, &c.

3 I'll go and tell him all I've done,
   Fall down before his face,
Unworthy to be called his son,
   I'll seek a servant's place.
      I'll die no more, &c.

4 His father saw him coming back,
   He saw, and ran, and smil'd,
And threw his arms around the neck
   Of his rebellious child.
      I'll die no more, &c.

5 Father, I've sinned, but O forgive!
   Enough, the Father said;
Rejoice, my house, my Son's alive,
   For whom I mourned as dead.
      I'll die no more, &c.

6 Now let the fatted calf be slain
   And spread the news around;
My son was dead and lives again;
   Was lost, but now is found.
      I'll die no more, &c.

7 'Tis thus the Lord his love reveals,
   To call poor sinners home;
More than a Father's love he feels,
   And welcomes all that come.
      I'll die no more, &c.

COME TO JESUS.

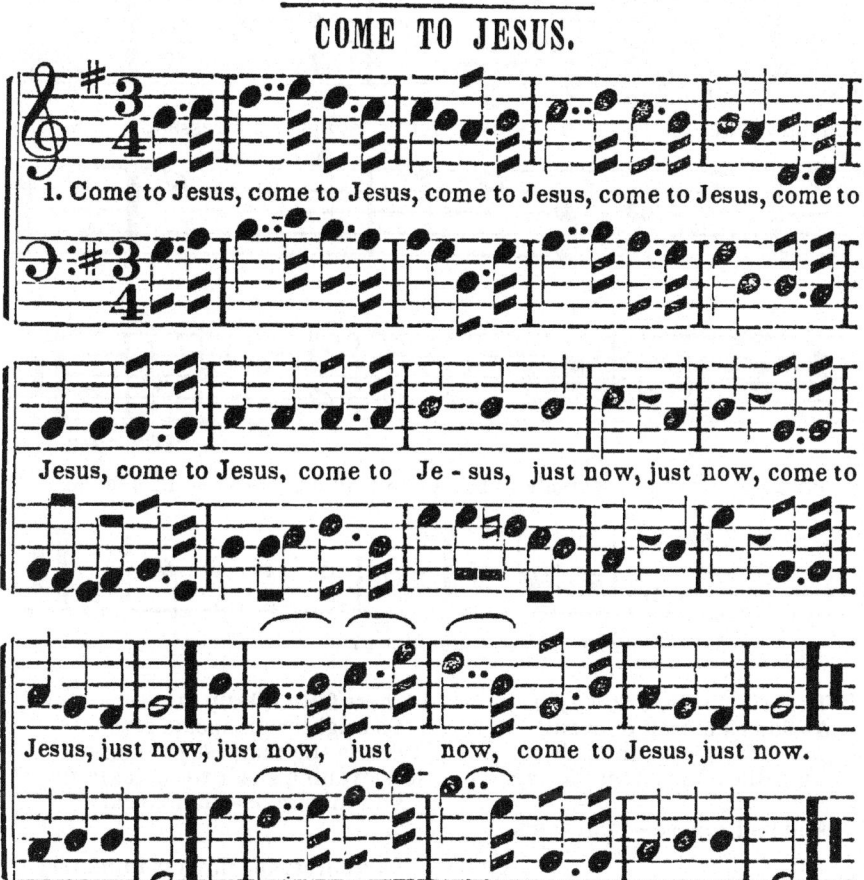

1. Come to Jesus, come to Jesus, come to Jesus, come to Jesus, come to Jesus, come to Jesus, come to Jesus, just now, just now, come to Jesus, just now, just now, just now, come to Jesus, just now.

2 He will save you—*just now.*
3 He is able—*just now.*
4 He is willing—*just now.*
5 He is ready—*just now.*
6 I believe it—*just now.*

7 Can you doubt him—*just now.*
8 See him pleading—*just now.*
9 Lo, he saves you—*just now.*
10 Hallelujah—*Amen.*

WOODLAND.* C. M.

NOTE.—*We hardly know an equal to the sweetness of the melody of this tune and words.*

* *From Church Harmony.*

2 There is a soft, a downy bed,
 As fair as breath of even;
A couch for weary mortals spread,
 Where they may rest the aching head,
 And find repose—in heaven.

3 There is a home for weary souls,
 By sin and sorrow driven;
Where tossed on life's tempestuous shoals,
Where storms arise and ocean rolls,
 And all is drear—but heaven.

4 There faith lifts up the tearless eye,
 To brighter prospects given;
It views the tempest passing by,
Sees evening shadows quickly fly,
 And all serene—in heaven.

5 There fragrant flowers immortal bloom,
 And joys supreme are given;
There rays divine disperse the gloom,
Beyond the dark and narrow tomb
 Appears the dawn of heaven

Nothing true but Heaven.

1 This world is all a fleeting show,
  For man's illusion given;
The smiles of joy, the tears of wo,
Deceitful shine, deceitful flow,
  There's nothing true but heaven.

2 And false the light on glory's plume,
  As fading hues of even;
And genius' bud and beauty's bloom
Are blossoms gathered for the tomb;
  There's nothing bright but heaven.

3 Poor wanderers of a stormy day,
  From wave to wave we're driven;
And fancy's flash and reason's ray,
Serve but to light the troubled way,
  There's nothing calm but heaven.

4 In vain do mortals sigh for bliss,
  Without their sins forgiven;
True pleasure, everlasting peace,
Are only found in God's free grace;
  There's nothing good but heaven.

The Perfect Heart.

1 O for a heart to praise my God,
  A heart from sin set free;
A heart that always feels thy blood,
  So freely spilt for me.

2 A heart resign'd, submissive, meek,
  My great Redeemer's throne;
Where only Christ is heard to speak,
  Where Jesus reigns alone.

3 O for a lowly contrite heart,
  Believing, true, and clean!
Which neither life nor death can part
  From him that dwells within.

4 A heart in every thought renew'd,
  And full of love divine;
Perfect, and right, and pure, and good,
  A copy, Lord, of thine.

5 Thy nature, gracious Lord, impart,
  Come quickly from above;
Write thy new name upon my heart,
  Thy new, best name of love.

Heaven on Earth.

1 This world's not " all a fleeting show,
  For man's illusion given;"
He that hath sooth'd a widow's wo,
Or wiped the orphan's tear, doth know
  There's something here of heaven.

2 And he that walks life's thorny way,
  With feelings calm and even;
Whose path is lit from day to day
By virtue's bright and steady ray,
  Hath something felt of heaven.

3 He that the Christian's course hath run,
  And all his foes forgiven—
Who measures out life's little span,
In love to God, and love to man,
  On earth has tasted heaven.

4 From such as walk in wisdom's road,
  Corroding fears are driven;
They're washed in Christ's atoning blood,
Enjoy communion with their God,
  And find their way to heaven.

The Watchful Heart.

1 I want a principle within,
  Of jealous, godly fear;
A sensibility of sin,
  A pain to feel it near;

2 I want the first approach to feel,
  Of pride, or fond desire;
To catch the wand'ring of my will,
  And quench the kindling fire.

3 From thee that I no more may part,
  No more thy goodness grieve,
The filial awe, the fleshly heart,
  The tender conscience give.

4 Quick as the apple of an eye,
  O God, my conscience make!
Awake my soul when sin is nigh,
  And keep it still awake.

5 If to the right or left I stray,
  That moment, Lord, reprove;
And let me weep my life away,
  For having griev'd thy love.

6 O may the least omission pain,
  My well-instructed soul!
And drive me to the blood again,
  Which makes the wounded whole.

2 Thy garden and thy pleasant walks,
  My study long have been;
Such dazzling views by human sight,
  Has never yet been seen.
If heaven be thus so glorious, Lord,
  Why should I stay from thence;
What folly's this that I should dread,
  To die and go from hence!

3 Reach down, O Lord, thine arm of grace,
  And cause me to ascend;
Where congregations ne'er break up,
  And sabbaths never end.
Jesus, my Lord, to glory's gone,
  Him will I go and see;
And all my brethren here below,
  Will soon come after me.

4 My friends, I bid you all adieu,
  I leave you in God's care,
And if I never more see you,
  Go on, I'll meet you there.
When we've been there ten thousand years,
  Bright shining as the sun,
We've no less days to sing God's praise,
  Than when we first begun.

Christian Fellowship.

1 Lift up your hearts to things above,
  Ye followers of the Lamb,
And join with us to praise his love,
  And glorify his name.
To Jesus' name give thanks and sing,
  Whose mercies never end:
Rejoice! rejoice! the Lord is King!
  The King is now our Friend!

2 We for his sake count all things loss,
  On earthly good look down;
And joyfully sustain the cross,
  Till we receive the crown.
O let us stir each other up,
  Our faith by works t'approve,
By holy purifying hope,
  And the sweet task of love.

The Christian's Hope.

1 How happy every child of grace,
  Who knows his sins forgiven!
This earth, he cries, is not my place,
  I seek my place in heaven;
A country far from mortal sight,
  Yet O! by faith I see;
The land of rest, the saints' delight,
  The heaven prepar'd for me.

2 O what a blessed hope is ours!
  While here on earth we stay,
We more than taste the heavenly powers,
  And antedate that day;
We feel the resurrection near,
  Our life in Christ conceal'd,
And with his glorious presence here
  Our earthen vessels fill'd.

Heaven Anticipated.

1 Arise, my soul, to Pisgah's height,
  And view the promised land;
And see by faith the glorious sight,
  Our heritage at hand;
A land where pure enjoyments dwell,
  And blessings most divine;
Where saints their highest notes do swell,
  And in bright glory shine.

2 There endless springs of pleasure flow,
  At my Redeemer's side,
For all who live by faith below,
  And in their Lord confide;
Fair Salem's dazzling gates are seen,
  Just o'er the narrow flood;
And fields, adorn'd with living green,
  The residence of God.

3 My conflicts here will soon be past,
  Where wild distraction reigns;
Through toil and death I'll reach at last,
  Fair Canaan's happy plains.
The lamp of life will soon grow pale,
  The spark will soon decay,
And then my happy soul will sail
  To everlasting day.

14. THE CHRISTIAN SOLDIER. C. M.

1. Am I a soldier of the cross, A follower of the Lamb?
And shall I fear to own his cause, Or blush to speak his name?

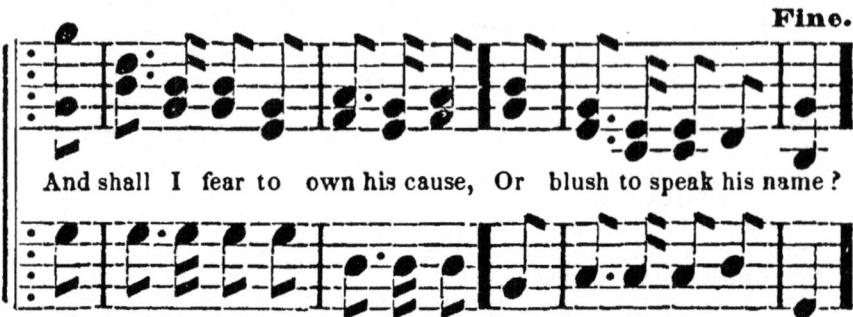

Whilst others fought to win the prize, And sail'd through bloody seas.

Must I be carried to the skies, On flow'ry beds of ease;

2 Are there no foes for me to face?
Must I not stem the flood?
Is this vile world a friend to grace,
To help me on to God?
Sure I must fight if I would reign,
Increase my courage, Lord.
I'll bear the toil, endure the pain,
Supported by thy word.

3 Thy saints in all this glorious war,
Shall conquer though they die;
They see the triumph from afar,
And seize it with their eye.
When that illustrious day shall rise,
And all thy armies shine
In robes of vict'ry through the skies,
The glory shall be thine.

BRIGHT CANAAN. C. M. J. B. PACKARD. 15

1. There is a land of pure delight, Where saints immortal reign,

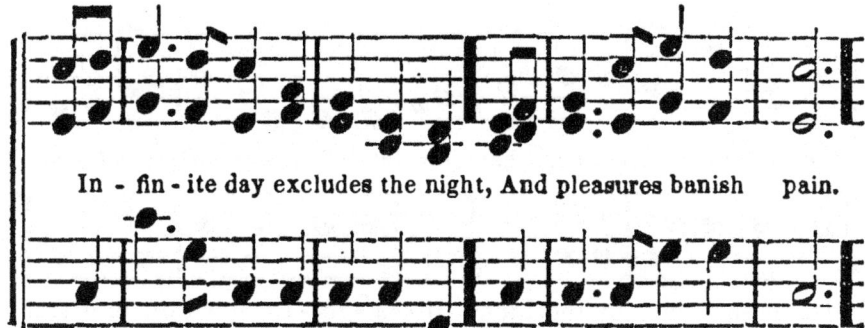

Infinite day excludes the night, And pleasures banish pain.

O Canaan, bright Canaan, It is the land of Canaan.

2 There everlasting spring abides,
　And never with'ring flowers,
Death, like a narrow sea, divides
　This heavenly land from ours.
　　O Canaan, &c.

3 Sweet fields beyond the swelling flood,
　Stand dressed in living green;
So to the Jews old Canaan stood,
　While Jordan rolled between,
　　O Canaan, &c.

4 Could we but climb where Moses stood,
　And view the landscape o'er;
Not Jordan's stream, nor death's cold flood,
　Should fright us from the shore.
　　O Canaan, &c

16 ADVENT. C. P. M.

From the Wesleyan Harp.

1. What sound is this salutes my ear? 'Tis
2. Behold the fair Jerusalem, Il-

Gabriel's trump methinks I hear, 'Tis Gabriel's trump methinks I hear,
luminated by the Lamb, Illuminated by the Lamb.

The expected day has come. Behold the heav'ns, the
In glory doth appear, Fair Zion rising

earth, the sea, Proclaim the year of Jubilee, Pro-
from the tombs, To meet the Bridegroom, lo! he comes, To

claim the year of Ju-bi-lee, Re-turn, ye ex-iles, home.

meet the Bridegroom, lo! he comes, And hails the festive year.

3 My soul is striving to be there;
I long to rise and wing the air,
  And trace the sacred road.
Adieu, adieu, all earthly things;
O that I had an angel's wings,
  I'd quickly see my God.

4 Fly, lingering moments, fly, O fly,
I thirst, I pant, I long to try,
  Angelic joys to prove!
Soon shall I quit this house of clay,
Clap my glad wings and soar away,
  And shout redeeming love.

The Savior's Love.

1
O Love divine, how sweet thou art:
When shall I find my willing heart
  All taken up by thee?
I thirst, I faint, I die to prove
The greatness of redeeming love,
  The love of Christ to me.

2
Stronger his love than death or hell,
Its riches are unsearchable;
  The first born sons of light
Desire in vain its depths to see:
They cannot reach the mystery,
  The length, the breadth, and height.

3
God only knows the love of God;
O that it now were shed abroad
  In this poor stony heart!
For love I sigh, for love I pine;
This only portion, Lord, be mine!
  Be mine this better part.

Excellency of Christ.

1
O could I speak the matchless worth,
Oh, could I sound the glories forth,
  Which in my Savior shine!
I'd soar and touch the heavenly strings,
And vie with Gabriel while he sings,
  In notes almost divine.

2
I'd sing the precious blood he spilt,
My ransom from the dreadful guilt
  Of sin and wrath divine:
I'd sing his glorious righteousness,
In which all perfect heavenly dress
  My soul shall ever shine.

3
I'd sing the characters he bears,
And all the forms of love he wears,
  Exalted on his throne:
In loftiest songs of sweetest praise,
I would, to everlasting days
  Make all his glories known.

4
Well, the delightful day will come
When my dear Lord will bring me home,
  And I shall see his face:
Then, with my Savior, brother, friend,
A blest eternity I'll spend,
  Triumphant in his grace.
    MEDLEY.

[2*]

WESLEYAN CHAPEL. C. P. M.

1. Come on my partners in distress, My comrades through this wilderness, Who still your bodies feel; Awhile forget your griefs and fears, And look beyond this vale of tears, To that celestial hill.

2
Beyond the bounds of time and space,
Look forward to that heavenly place,
  The saint's secure abode;
On faith's strong eagle pinions rise,
And force your passage to the skies,
  And scale the mount of God.

3
Who suffer with our Master here,
We shall before his face appear,
  And by his side sit down;
To patient faith the prize is sure,
And all who to the end endure
  The cross, shall wear the crown.

4
Thrice blessed, bliss inspiring hope
It lifts the fainting spirit up;
  It brings to life the dead.
Our conflicts here shall soon be past,
And you and I ascend at last,
  Triumphant, with our Head.

5
In hope of that ecstatic pause,
Jesus, we now sustain the cross,
  And at thy footstool fall;
Till thou our hidden life reveal—
Till thou our ravished spirits fill—
  And God be all in all.—

The Glorious Hope.

1
O glorious hope of perfect love !
It lifts me up to things above !
  It bears on eagles' wings ;
It gives my ravish'd soul to taste,
And makes me for some moments feast,
  With Jesus' priests and kings.

2
There is my house and portion fair,
My treasure and my heart is there,
  And my abiding home.
For me my elder brethren stay,
And angels beckon me away,
  And Jesus bids me come !

3
I come, thy servant, Lord, replies,
I come to meet thee in the skies,
  And claim my heavenly rest ;
Now let the pilgrim's journey end,
Now, O my Savior, brother, friend,
  Receive me to thy breast !

Prospect of Eternity.

1
Lo ! on a narrow neck of land,
'Twixt two unbounded seas I stand,
  Secure, insensible ;
A point of time, a moment's space,
Removes me to that heavenly place,
  Or shuts me up in hell.

2
O God, mine inmost soul convert,
And deeply on my thoughtful heart
  Eternal things impress ;
Give me to feel their solemn weight,
And tremble on the brink of fate,
  And wake to righteousness !

3
Before me place in dread array,
The pomp of that tremendous day,
  When thou with clouds shalt come,
To judge the nations at thy bar,
And tell me, Lord, shall I be there,
  To meet a joyful doom !

The Good Resolve.

1
Be it my only wisdom here,
To serve the Lord with filial fear,
  With loving gratitude ;
Superior sense may I display,
By shunning every evil way,
  And walking in the good.

2
O may I still from sin depart ;
A wise and understanding heart,
  Jesus, to me be given !
And let me through thy spirit know,
To glorify my God below,
  And find my way to heaven.

The Solemn Inquiry.

1
And am I only born to die ?
And must I suddenly comply
  With nature's stern decree ?
What after death for me remains ?
Celestial joys, or hellish pains,
  To all eternity !

2
How then ought I on earth to live,
While God prolongs the kind reprieve
  And props the house of clay ;
My sole concern, my single care,
To watch, and tremble, and prepare
  Against that fatal day !

3
No room for mirth or trifling here
For worldly hope, or worldly fear,
  If life so soon is gone ;
If now the Judge is at the door,
And all mankind must stand before
  Th' inexorable throne !

4
No matter which my thoughts em-
A moment's misery or joy ;   (ploy,
  But O ! when both shall end,
Where shall I find my destin'd place?
Shall I my everlasting days,
  With fiends or angels spend ?

5
Nothing is worth a thought beneath
But how I may escape the death
  That never, never dies !
How make mine own election sure ;
And when I fail on earth, secure
  A mansion in the skies.

2
This song repeat, repeat, ye saints in glory,
God is Love!
And saints on earth shout back the pleasing story,
God is Love!
In this let earth and heaven agree,
To sound his love both full and free,
And let the theme forever be,
God is Love!

3
Creation speaks with thousand tongues proclaiming,
God is Love!
And Providence unites her voice exclaiming,
God is Love!
But let the burdened sinner hear
The Gospel, sounding loud and clear,
To every soul both far and near,
God is Love!

4
This heavenly love all round is sweetly flowing,
God is Love!
And in my heart the sacred fire is glowing,
God is Love!
That God is love I know full well;
And had I power his love to tell,
With loudest notes my song should swell:
God is Love!

5
The love of God is now my greatest pleasure,
God is Love!
And while I live, I'll ask no other treasure,
God is Love!
This theme shall be my song below,
And when to glory I shall go,
This strain eternally shall flow,—
God is Love! S. LOVELL.

All is Well.

1
What's this that steals, that steals upon my frame?
Is it death?
That soon will quench, will quench this vital flame,
Is it death?
If this be death, I soon shall be
From every pain and sorrow free,
I shall the King of glory see,
All is well.

2
Weep not, my friends, my friends, weep not for me.
All is well.
My sins are pardoned, pardoned, I am free,
All is well.
There's not a cloud that doth arise,
To hide my Savior from my eyes.
I soon shall mount the upper skies.
All is well.

3
Tune, tune your harps, your harps, ye saints in glory.
All is well.
I will rehearse, rehearse the pleasing story,
All is well.
Bright angels are from glory come,
They're round my bed, they're in my room,
They wait to waft my spirit home.
All is well.

4
Hark, hark! my Lord, my Lord and Master calls me.
All is well.
I soon shall see, shall see his face in glory.
All is well.
Farewell, dear friends, adieu, adieu!
I can no longer stay with you.
My glittering crown appears in view.
All is well.

22 MILLENNIAL DAWN. 7s & 6s.
G. J. WEBB.

NOTE.—*The very extended use of this tune for the past year, is the best evidence of its value.*

1. The morning light is breaking, The darkness disappears,
2. Rich dews of grace come o'er us, In many a gentle shower,

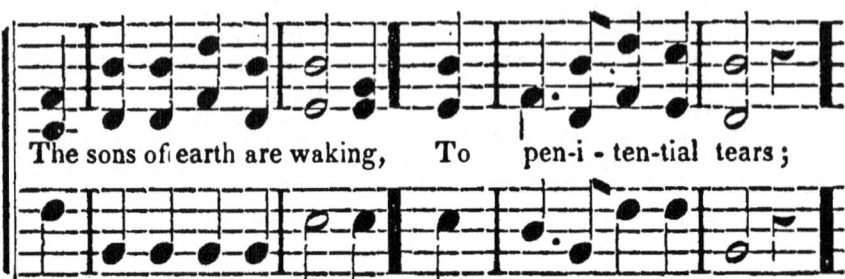

The sons of earth are waking, To pen-i-ten-tial tears;
And brighter scenes before us, Are opening every hour;

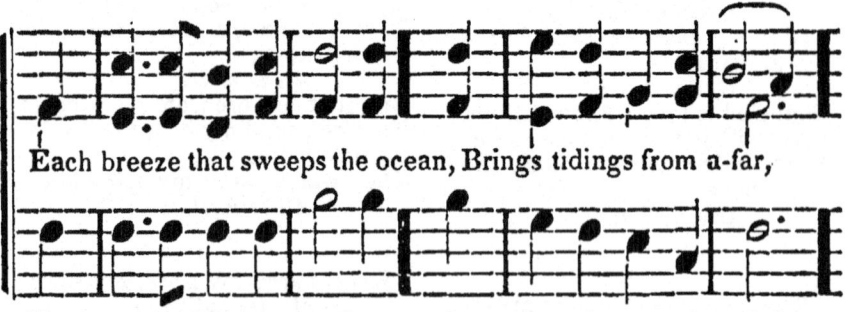

Each breeze that sweeps the ocean, Brings tidings from a-far,
Each cry to Heaven go-ing, A-bun-dant answers brings,

Of nations in commotion, Prepared for Zion's war.
And heavenly gales are blowing, With peace upon their wings

3 See heathen nations bending,
  Before the God we love!
And thousand hearts ascending
  In gratitude above;
While sinners now confessing,
  The gospel call obey,
And seek the Savior's blessing,
  A nation in a day.
4 Blest river of salvation,
  Pursue thy onward way,
Flow thou to every nation,
  Nor in thy richness stay;
Stay not, till all the lowly,
  Triumphant reach their home,
Stay not, till all the holy,
  Proclaim, the Lord has come.

Go into every nation.
1 From heaven's blissful regions,
  Where seraphs dwell in light,
Where many shining legions
  Of spirits clad in white,
The Prince of Life descended,
  To save a fallen race,
Who had their Lord offended,
  And forfeited his grace.
2 We'll hail him as our Savior,
  And fall upon his arms;
We'll thank him for the favor,
  And dwell upon his charms:
We'll raise our joyful voices,
  His sovereign grace to sing;
While many a heart rejoices
  To welcome him their King.
3 "Go into every nation,"
  We hear him loud proclaim;
"Publish to them salvation;
  Go, preach it in my name."
We'll tell the pleasing story
  Which saints rehearse above,
Who reign with him in glory,
  And dwell upon his love.
4 While we our anthems tender
  Unto the Prince of Peace,
He shall, with royal splendor,
  The heathen's light increase;
Till, beauteous, on their mountains,
  The trumpeters shall stand,
And Zion's blissful fountains,
  Stream gladness through the land.

The Patience of Hope.
1 Oh, when shall I see Jesus,
  And reign with him above,
And from that flowing fountain
  Drink everlasting love!
When shall I be delivered
  From this vain world of sin,
And with my blessed Jesus
  Drink endless pleasures in?
2 Through grace I am determined
  To conquer though I die;
And then away to Jesus
  On wings of love I'll fly.
Farewell to sin and sorrow,
  I bid you all adieu;
And, O, my friends, be faithful,
  And on your way pursue.
3 And if you meet with troubles
  And trials on your way,
Then cast your care on Jesus,
  And don't forget to pray
Gird on the heavenly armor
  Of faith, and hope, and love,
And when the combat's ended,
  He'll carry you above.

The Great Physician.
1 How lost was my condition
  Till Jesus made me whole!
There is but one Physician
  Can cure the sin sick soul!
Next door to death he found me,
  And snatched me from the grave,
To tell to all around me,
  His wondrous power to save.
2 From men great skill professing,
  I thought a cure to gain;
But this proved more distressing,
  And added to my pain;
Some said that nothing ail'd me,
  Some gave me up for lost;
Thus every refuge fail'd me,
  And all my hopes were cross'd.
3 At length this great Physician,
  (How matchless is his grace!)
Accepted my petition,
  And undertook my case:
He gave me sight to view him,
  For sin my eyes had sealed;
Then bade me look upon him.
  I looked, and I was heal'd.

24. EXPOSTULATION. 11s.

NOTE.—*This hymn and tune are well calculated to arrest the sinner in sin and lead him to Christ.*

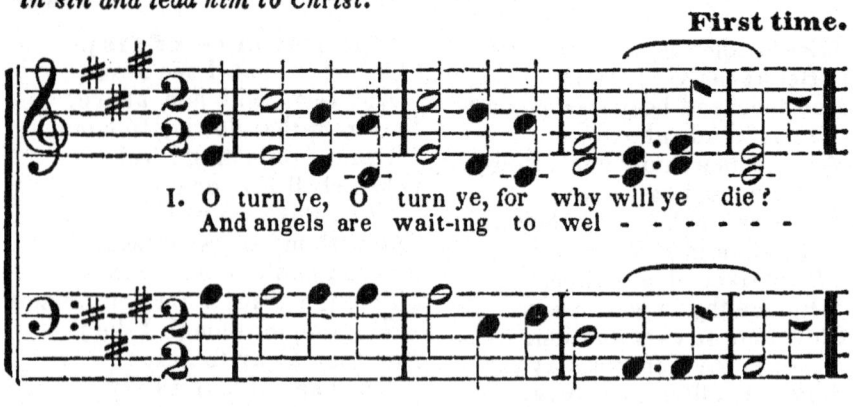

1. O turn ye, O turn ye, for why will ye die?
And angels are wait-ing to wel- - - - - -come you home.

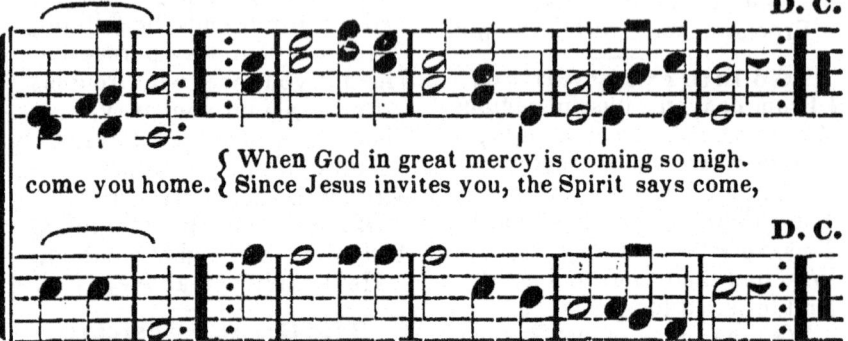

{ When God in great mercy is coming so nigh.
  Since Jesus invites you, the Spirit says come,

2 How vain the delusion, that while you delay,
Your hearts may grow better by staying away ;
Come wretched, come starving, come just as you be,
While streams of salvation are flowing so free.

3 And now Christ is ready your souls to receive,
O how can you question, if you will believe ;
If sin is your burden, why will you not come,
'Tis you he bids welcome ; he bids you come home.

4 In riches, in pleasures, what can you obtain,
To soothe your affliction, or banish your pain !
To bear up your Spirit when summon'd to die,
Or waft you to mansions of glory on high.

5 Why will you be starving and feeding on air ?
There's mercy in Jesus, enough and to spare ;
If still you are doubting, make trial and see,
And prove that his mercy is boundless and free.

6 Come, give us your hand, and the Savior your heart,
And trusting in heaven we never shall part ;
O, how can we leave you ? why will you not come ?
We'll journey together, and soon be at home

PARADISE. C. P. M.

1. The Lord in-to his garden comes, The spices yield a

rich perfume, The lilies grow and thrive, The lilies grow and thrive;

Refreshing show'rs of grace divine, From Jesus flows to every vine, And

makes the dead re-vive, And makes the dead re-vive.

2 This makes the dry and barren ground,
In springs of water to abound,
  And fruitful soil become;
The desert blossoms like the rose,
When Jesus conquers all his foes,
  And makes his people one.

3 The glorious time is rolling on,
The gracious work is now begun,
  My soul a witness is;
Come, taste and see the pardon free
To all mankind, as well as me;
  Who come to Christ may live.

4 We feel that heaven is now begun,
It issues from a shining throne,
  From Jesus' throne on high;
It comes like floods we can't contain,
We drink, and drink, and drink again;
  And yet for more we cry.

5 But when we come to reign above,
And all surround the throne of love,
  We'll drink a full supply;
Jesus will lead his armies thro',
To living fountains where they flow,
  That never will run dry.

6 There we shall reign, and shout and sing,
And make the upper regions ring,
  When all the saints get home;
Come on, come on, my brethren dear,
Soon we shall meet together there,
  For Jesus bids us come.

2 Here I'll raise mine Ebenezer,
   Hither by thy help I'm come;
  And I hope, by thy good pleasure,
   Safely to arrive at home.
  Jesus sought me when a stranger,
   Wand'ring from the fold of God;
  He, to rescue me from danger,
   Interpos'd his precious blood!
        Glory, &c.

3 O! to grace how great a debtor
   Daily I'm constrain'd to be?
  Let thy goodness, like a fetter,
   Bind my wand'ring heart to thee:
  Prone to wander, Lord, I feel it;
   Prone to leave the God I love—
  Here's my heart, O take and seal it;
   Seal it for thy courts above.
        Glory, &c.

The Savior born.

1
Hark! what mean those holy voices,
Sweetly sounding through the skies?
Lo! th' angelic host rejoices;
Heavenly hallelujah's rise.
Hark! the heralds of salvation!
Joyful news the angels bring;
God, himself in flesh hath entered,
Jesus is the new born King!
   Glory, &c.

2
Hear them tell the wondrous story,
Hear them chant in hymns of joy,
"Glory in the highest—glory!
Glory be to God most high!
Peace on earth—good will from heaven,
Reaching far as man is found.
Souls redeemed, and sins forgiven,"
Loud our golden harps shall sound.
   Glory, &c.

3
Christ is born, the great Anointed;
Heaven and earth his praises sing!
Oh receive whom God appointed,
For your Prophet, Priest and King.
Haste, ye mortals to adore him;
Learn his name and taste his joy;
Till in heaven ye sing before him,
Glory be to God most high!
   Glory, &c.   CAWOOD.

Full Salvation.

1 Love divine, all loves excelling,
  Joy of heaven to earth come down;
  Fix in us thy humble dwelling,
  All thy faithful mercies crown!
  Jesus, thou art all compassion,
  Pure unbounded love thou art;
  Visit us with thy salvation,
  Enter every trembling heart.
        Glory, &c.

2 Breathe, O breathe thy loving Spirit,
  Into every troubled breast!
  Let us all in thee inherit,
  Let us find that second rest.
  Take away our bent of sinning,
  Alpha and Omega be,
  End of faith as its beginning,
  Set our hearts at liberty
        Glory, &c.

3 Come, Almighty to deliver,
  Let us all thy life receive,
  Suddenly return, and never,
  Never more thy temples leave
  Thee we would be always blessing,
  Serve thee as thy hosts above,
  Pray, and praise thee without ceasing,
  Glory in thy perfect love.
        Glory, &c.

4 Finish then thy new creation,
  Pure and spotless let us be;
  Let us see thy great salvation,
  Perfectly restor'd in thee:
  Chang'd from glory into glory,
  Till in heaven we take our place,
  Till we cast our crowns before thee,
  Lost in wonder, love, and praise!
        Glory, &c.

Doxology.

Glory, honor, power, and blessing,
Be unto the Father given:
Sing his praises without ceasing,
Sons of earth, and hosts of heaven.
Glory be to Christ the Savior,
Who hath bought us with his blood;
Glory to the blessed Spirit,
Glory to the mighty God.
        Glory, &c.

28 DISCIPLE. 8 & 7.

NOTE.—*A young lady in England, was much persecuted by her unconverted father, because she had embraced Jesus. He sought to divert her mind, and gave her a song to play and sing, called 'GO FORGET ME, WHY SHOULD SORROW &C,'—To his surprise she played and sung the following.*

1. Je-sus, I my cross have ta--ken, All to leave and fol-low thee, Na-ked, poor, de-spised, for-sa-ken, Thou, from hence my all shalt be. Per-ish ev'ry fond am-bi-tion,

All I've sought, or hoped, or known, Yet how rich is

my con-di-tion, God and heaven are still my own.

2
Let the world despise and leave me ;
They have left my Savior too ;
Human hearts and looks deceive me,
Thou art not, like them, untrue ;
And while thou shalt smile upon me,
God of wisdom, love, and might,
Foes may hate, and friends disown me ;
Show thy face, and all is bright

3
Go then, earthly fame and treasure,
Come, disaster, scorn and pain,
In thy service pain is pleasure,
With thy favor, loss is gain.
I have called thee Abba, Father,
I have set my heart on thee ;
Storms may howl, and clouds may gather,
All must work for good to me.

4
Haste thee on from grace to glory,
Armed by faith, and winged by prayer,
Heaven's eternal days before thee,
God's own hand shall guide thee there.
Soon shall close thy earthly mission,
Soon shall pass thy pilgrim days,
Hope shall change to glad fruition,
Faith to sight, and prayer to praise.

The foot of the Cross.

1
Sweet the moments, rich in blessing,
Which before the cross I spend ;
Life and health and peace possessing,
From the sinner's dying Friend.
Love and grief my heart dividing,
With my tears his feet I'll bathe ;
Still in faith and hope abiding,
Life deriving from his death.

2
O how blessed is this station,
Low before the cross I'll lie,
While I see divine compassion
Pleading in the Victim's eye ;
Here I'll sit forever viewing
Mercy streaming in his blood :
Precious drops, my soul bedewing,
Plead and claim my peace with God.

3
Here it is I find my heaven,
While upon the Lamb I gaze ;
Here I see my sins forgiven—
Lost in wonder, love and praise.
May I still enjoy this feeling,
In all need to Jesus go :
Prove his blood each day more healing,
And himself more deeply know.
ROBINSON

THE SAINT'S HOME. 11s.

NOTE.—*This tune is too good, and too general a favorite to be omitted in such a work as this.*

1. 'Mid scenes of confusion and creature complaints, How

sweet to my soul is com-mun-ion with saints? To find at the

banquet of mer-cy there's room, And feel in the presence of

Je-sus at home. *Home, home, sweet, sweet home, Pre-*

pare me, dear Savior, for glo-ry, my home.

2 An alien from God, and a stranger to grace,
I wandered through earth, its gay pleasures to trace,
In the pathway of sin I continued to roam,
Unmindful, alas! that it led me from home. *Home, &c.*

3 The pleasures of earth, I have seen fade away,
They bloom for a season, but soon they decay,
But pleasures more lasting, in Jesus are given,
Salvation on earth, and a mansion in heaven. *Home, &c.*

4 Allure me no longer, ye false glowing charms!
The Savior invites me, I'll go to his arms;
At the banquet of mercy, I hear there is room,
O there may I feast with his children at home! *Home, &c.*

I have started for Canaan.

Rev. S. Hoyt.

1 I have started for Canaan, must I leave you behind?
Will you not go up with me? come make up your mind.
The land lies before us, 'tis pleasant to view;
Its fruits are abundant, they are offer'd to you.
    *Come, come, friends, friends, come,
    I've started for Canaan, Oh! will you not come?*

2 What can tempt you to linger, or turn from the way?
The fields are all blooming, as blooming as May.
The music is charming, the harmony pure;
The joys there are lasting, they ever endure.
    Come, &c.

3 You have friends in that country, most dear to your heart,
Do you not wish to meet them, where friends never part?
Then start in a moment, no longer delay,
While you stop to consider, the night ends the day.
    Come, &c.

4 'Tis the last call of mercy, oh! turn, lest you die,
Give your heart to the Savior, to-day he is nigh.
While his arms are extended, while his children all pray,
Will you not join our number? come, join us to-day.
    Come, &c.

JESUS REIGNS.

Arranged for this work.

1. Earth, re-joice, our Lord is King! Sons of men, his praises sing;

Sing ye in triumphant strains, Jesus our Mes-si-ah reigns!

Oh, ride on, Je - - sus, Oh ride on!

2 Power is all to Jesus given,
Lord of hell, and earth, and heaven!
Every knee to him shall bow;
Satan, hear, and tremble now!
   Oh, ride on, &c.

3 Angels and archangels join,
All triumphantly combine;
All in Jesus' praise agree,
Carrying on his victory.
   Oh, ride on, &c.

4 Though the sons of night blaspheme,
More there are with us than them;
God with us, we cannot fear,
Fear, ye fiends, for Christ is here!
   Oh, ride on, &c.

5 Our Messiah is come down,
Claims the nations for his own,
Bids them stand before his face,
Triumphant in his saving grace.
   Oh, ride on, &c.

BEHOLD I BRING YOU GOOD TIDINGS. 33

1. Hail the blest morn! see the great Mediator, Down from the
regions of glory descend!
Shepherds, go worship the babe in the manger; Lo! for his
guard the bright angels attend.

FINE.

An-gels a-dore him in slumbers reclining, Wise men and
shepherds before him do fall

Cold on his cra-dle the dew drops are shining, Low lies his head with the beasts of the stall.

D. C.

2 Say, shall we yield him in costly devotion,
   Odors of Eden, and offerings divine,
Gems from the mountain, and pearls from the ocean,
   Myrrh from the forest, and gold from the mine?
Vainly we offer each ample oblation,
   Vainly with gold we his favor secure;
Richer by far is the heart's adoration;
   Dearer to God are the prayers of the poor.

CHORUS.
Brightest and best of the sons of the morning,
   Dawn on our darkness, and lend us thine aid;
Star in the east, the horizon adorning,
   Guide where our infant Redeemer was laid.

SHOUTING VICTORY.

Arranged for this work.

1. When I can read my ti-tle clear, To man-sions in the skies, I'll bid farewell to ev'-ry fear, And wipe my weeping eyes. *Shouting vic-to-ry, vic-to-ry, vic-t'ry o-ver death, Shouting vic-to-ry, vic-to-ry, I long to see that day.*

quick.

2 Should earth against my soul engage,
And fiery darts be hurl'd,
Then I can smile at Satan's rage,
And face a frowning world.
Shouting victory, &c.

3 Let cares like a wild deluge come,
Let storms of sorrow fall;
So I but safely reach my home,
My God, my heaven, my all
Shouting victory &c.

4 There I shall bathe my weary soul,
In seas of heavenly rest,
And not a wave of trouble roll
Across my peaceful breast.
Shouting victory, &c.

THE CHRISTIAN'S TRIUMPH. 7s.

Arranged for this work.

1. Children of the heavenly King, As we journey let us sing;
Sing our Savior's worthy praise, Glorious in his works and ways.
Oh how happy we shall be, When we've gained the victory.
vic-to-ry, vic-to-ry, When we've gained the victory.

2 We are traveling home to God,
In the way our fathers trod;
They are happy now, and we
Soon their happiness shall see.
Victory, &c.

3 O ye banished seed be glad,
Christ our advocate is made;
Us to save our flesh assumes,
Brother to our souls becomes.
Victory, &c.

4 Fear not, brethren, joyful stand
On the borders of our land;
Jesus Christ, our Father's Son,
Bids us undismay'd go on.
Victory, &c.

5 Lord! obediently we'll go,
Gladly leaving all below;
Only thou our leader be,
And we still will follow thee!
Victory, &c.

LO, I AM WITH YOU. 11s.

1. The Lord is our shepherd, our guardian and guide;
   Whatever we want, he will kindly provide,
   To sheep of his pasture, his mercies abound,
   His care and protection, his flock will surround.

2. The Lord is our shepherd, what then shall we fear,
   What danger can move us, while Jesus is near?
   Not when the time calls us to walk through the vale
   Of the shadow of death, shall our hearts ever fail

3 In ev'ry condition—in sickness, in health,
In poverty's vale, or abounding in wealth,
At home and abroad, on the land, on the sea,
As thy days may demand, so thy succor shall be.

4 "Fear not, I am with thee; O be not dismay'd!
For I am thy God, and will still give thee aid;
I'll strengthen thee, help thee, and cause thee to stand,
Upheld by my righteous, Omnipotent hand.

5 "The soul that on Jesus hath leaned for repose,
I will not, I cannot desert to his foes;
That soul, though all hell should endeavor to shake,
I'll never—no, never—no, never forsake!"

Kedron.

1 Thou sweet gliding Kedron, by thy silver streams,
Our Savior at midnight, when moonlight's pale beams
Shone bright on the waters, would frequently stray,
And lose, in thy murmurs, the toils of the day.

2 How damp were the vapors that fell on his head!
How hard was his pillow, how humble his bed!
The angels, astonish'd, grew sad at the sight,
And follow'd their Master with solemn delight

3 O garden of Olivet, thou dear honor'd spot,
The fame of thy wonder shall ne'er be forgot;
The theme most transporting to seraphs above;
The triumph of sorrow, the triumph of love.

4 Come, saints, and adore him; come, bow at his feet!
O, give him the glory, the praise that is meet,
Let joyful hosannas unceasing arise,
And join the full chorus, that gladdens the skies.

I would not live alway.

1 I would not live alway: I ask not to stay,
Where storm after storm rises dark o'er the way,
The few lurid mornings that dawn on us here,
Are enough for life's woes, full enough for its cheer.

2 I would not live alway; no—welcome the tomb,
Since Jesus hath lain there, I dread not its gloom:
There, sweet be my rest, till he bid me arise
To hail him in triumph descending the skies.

3 Who, who would live alway, away from his God;
Away from yon heaven, that blissful abode,
Where the rivers of pleasure flow o'er the bright plains,
And the noontide of glory eternally reigns!

4 Where the saints of all ages in harmony meet,
Their Savior and brethren, transported to greet;
While the anthems of rapture unceasingly roll,
And the smile of the Lord is the feast of the soul.

38 CANAAN. L. M.

Arranged for this work.

NOTE.—*We are indebted for this tune to Rev. J. N. Maffitt, who first introduced it into this community.*—BOSTON.

1. How hap-py is the pil-grim's lot, } I am
   How free from ev-ery anx-ious thought, }
   bound for th' land of Canaan, Oh Ca-naan, bright Ca-naan, I am bound for the land of Canaan; O Canaan, it is my hap-py home, I am bound for the land of Canaan.

2 Nothing on earth I call my own,
  I'm bound, &c.
  A stranger to the world unknown,
  I'm bound, &c.
    Oh Canaan, &c.

3 I trample on their whole delight,
  I'm bound, &c.
  And seek a city out of sight,
  I'm bound, &c.
    Oh Canaan, &c.

4 There is my house and portion fair,
  I'm bound, &c.
  My treasure and my heart are there,
  I'm bound, &c.
    Oh Canaan, &c.

5 If you get there before I do,
  I'm bound, &c.
  Look out for me, I'm coming too,
  I'm bound, &c.
    Oh Canaan, &c.

6 I have some friends before me gone,
  I'm bound, &c.
  And I'm resolved to travel on,
  I'm bound, &c.
    Oh Canaan, &c.

7 Our songs of praise, shall fill the (skies,
  I'm bound, &c.
  While higher still our joys they rise,
  I'm bound, &c.
    Oh Canaan, &c.

There are angels hovering round.

Arranged for this work.

NOTE.—*How often has this short tune inspired the whole company when sung as sinners were turning to the Lord or Christians were rejoicing.*

1. There are an-gels hovering round, There are angels hovering round, There are an-gels, an-gels hovering round.

To carry the tidings home,
To the new Jerusalem;
Poor sinners are coming home,
And Jesus bids them come;
Let him that heareth come,
Let him that thirsteth come.

We are on our journey home.
Where Christ our Lord has gone.
We will meet around his throne.
When he makes his people one.
We shall reign forevermore.
In the new Jerusalem.

40 WILL YOU GO? 8s.

NOTE.—*This tune is full of earnestness and should be sung with strong feeling.*

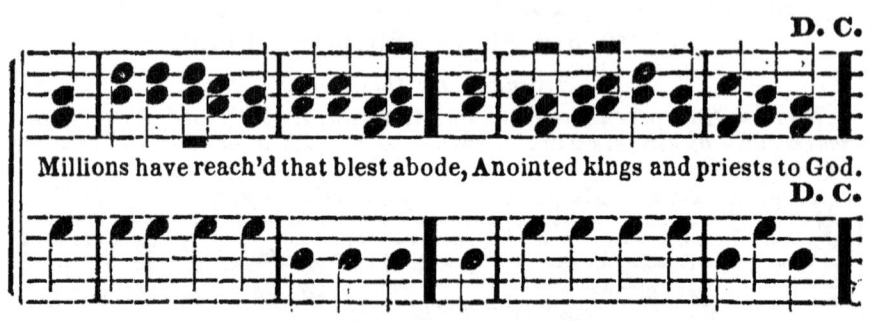

1. We're trav'ling home to Heav'n above, *Will you go? Will you go?*
To sing the Savior's dying love, *Will you go? Will you go?*
And millions more are on the road, *Will you go? Will you go?*
Millions have reach'd that blest abode, Anointed kings and priests to God.
D. C.

2 We're going to see the bleeding Lamb,
In rapturous strains to praise his name,
The crown of life we there shall wear,
The conqueror's palms our hands shall bear,
And all the joys of Heaven we'll share.
Will you go? &c.

3 We're going to join the Heavenly Choir,
To raise our voice and tune the lyre;
There saints and angels gladly sing,
Hosanna to their God and King,
And make the heavenly arches ring.
Will you go? &c.

4 Ye weary, heavy laden come,
In the blest house there still is room,
The Lord is waiting to receive,
If thou wilt on him now believe,
He'll give thy troubled conscience ease.
Will you go? &c.

5 The way to Heaven is free for all,
For Jew and Gentile, great and small,
Make up your mind, give God your heart,
With every sin and idol part,
And now for glory make a start.
Will you go? &c.

6 The way to Heaven is straight and plain,
Repent, believe, be born again,
The Savior cries aloud to thee,
"Take up thy cross and follow me,"
And thou shalt my salvation see.
Will you go? &c.

7 O, could I hear some sinner say,
I will go! I will go!
I'll start this moment, clear the way,
Let me go! Let me go!
My old companions, fare you well,
I will not go with you to hell,
I mean with Jesus Christ to dwell.
Let me go! Let me go!

RAPTURE OF LOVE. 6s & 9s.

NOTE.—*How truly is the experience of the faithful Christian related in the Hymn of this tune.*

1. O how happy are they Who their Savior obey, And have laid up their treasure a-bove! Tongue can never express The sweet com-fort and peace, Of a soul in its ear-li-est love.

2 That sweet comfort was mine,
  When the favor divine
    I first found in the blood of the Lamb,
  When my heart it believed,
  What a joy I received,
    What a heaven in Jesus' name.

3 'Twas a heaven below
  My Redeemer to know,
    And the angels could do nothing more,
  Than to fall at his feet,
  And the story repeat,
    And the lover of sinners adore.

4 Jesus all the day long
  Was my joy and my song;
    O that all his salvation might see,
  He hath loved me, I cried,
  He hath suffered and died,
    To redeem such a rebel as me.

5 O the rapturous height
  Of that holy delight
    Which I felt in the life-giving blood!
  Of my Savior possest,
  I was perfectly blest,
    As if filled with the goodness of God.

THE CONTRAST. P. M.

Not too fast.

1. I have sought round the verdant earth, For unfading joy;
I have tried ev'ry source of mirth, But all, all will cloy.
Lord, bestow on me, Grace to set the spirit free;
Thine the praise shall be; Mine, mine the joy.

2 I have wandered in mazes dark, Of doubt and distress,
I have had not a kindling spark, My spirit to bless;
Cheerless unbelief, Fill'd my laboring soul with grief,
What shall give relief? What shall give peace?

3 I then turned to thy Gospel, Lord, From folly away,
I then trusted thy holy word, That taught me to pray,
Here I found release. Weary spirit here found rest,
Hope of endless bliss, Eternal day.

4 I will praise now my Heavenly King, I'll praise and adore;
The heart's richest tribute bring To thee, God of power;
And in heaven above, Saved by thy redeeming love,
Loud the strains shall move, Forevermore

THE PENSIVE DOVE. C. M.

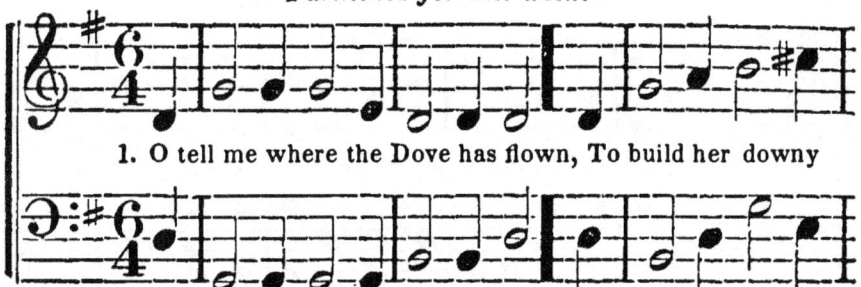

Furnished for this work.

1. O tell me where the Dove has flown, To build her downy nest; And I will rove this world all o'er, To win her to my breast; To win her to my breast.

2. I sought her in the groves of love, I knew her tender heart; But she had flown! the Pensive Dove Had felt a traitor's dart, Had felt a traitor's dart.

3 I sought her on the flowry lawn,
　Where pleasure holds her train;
But fancy flies from flower to
　　flower,
　So there I sought in vain.

4 'Twas on Ambition's craggy hill,
　The Pensive bird might stray;
I sought her there, though vainly
　　still;
　She never flew that way.

5 Faith smiled and shed a silent tear
　To see my search around,
Then whispered, "I will tell you
　　where
　"The Dove may yet be found.

6 " By *meek religion's humble cot*,
　"She builds her downy nest;
" Go seek that sweet secluded
　　spot,
　"And win her to your breast."

LANGTREE. C. M.

From Wesleyan Harp.

1. Jerusalem, my happy home, When shall I go to thee?
When will my labors have an end, Thy joys when shall I see?
When shall these eyes thy heaven-built walls, And pearly gates behold?
Thy bulwarks with salvation crowned, And streets of shining gold?

2 O when thou city of my God,
  Shall I thy courts ascend,
Where congregations ne'er break up,
  And Sabbaths never end?
Why should I shrink from pain and wo,
  Or feel at death, dismay?
Jerusalem, I soon shall view,
  In realms of endless day.

3 We there shall meet, no more to part,
  And heaven shall ring with praise;
While Jesus's love in every heart,
  Shall tune the song—free grace.
Jerusalem, my happy home,
  O how I long for thee;
My sorrows all shall have an end,
  When once thy joys I see.

I shall be holy here.

1 O joyful sound of Gospel grace!
Christ shall in me appear!
I, even I, shall see his face;
I shall be holy here.
The glorious crown of right'ousness
To me reach'd out I view;
Conqu'ror through him I soon shall seize,
And wear it as my due.

2 The promis'd land, from Pisgab's top,
I now exult to see;
My hope is full (O glorious hope!)
Of immortality.
He visits now the house of clay;
He shakes his future home;
O wouldst thou, Lord, on this glad day,
Into thy temple come!

3 With me, I know, I feel thou art;
But this cannot suffice,
Unless thou plantest in my heart
A constant paradise.
Come, O my God, thyself reveal,
Fill all this mighty void;
Thou only canst my spirit fill;
Come, O my God, my God!

The Sanctified heart.

1 My God, I know, I feel thee mine,
And will not quit my claim,
Till all I have is lost in thine,
And all renew'd I am.
I hold thee with a trembling hand,
And will not let thee go,
Till steadfastly by faith I stand,
And all thy goodness know.

2 Jesus, thine all victorious love
Shed in my heart abroad
Then shall my feet no longer rove,
Rooted and fix'd in God.
O that in me the sacred fire,
Might now begin to glow!
Burn up the dross of base desire,
And make the mountains flow!

3 O that it now from heaven might fall,
And all my sins consume:
Come, Holy Ghost, for thee I call,
Spirit of burning, come.
Refining fire, go through my heart,
Illuminate my soul;
Scatter thy life through every part,
And sanctify the whole.

Prospect of Heaven.

1 My span of life will soon be done,
The passing moments say;
As length'ning shadows o'er the mead,
Proclaim the close of day.
O that my heart might dwell aloof,
From all created things,
And learn that wisdom from above
Whence true contentment springs.

2 Courage, my soul, thy bitter cross
In every trial here,
Shall bear thee to thy heaven above,
But shall not enter there.
The sighing ones that humbly seek
In sorrowing paths below,
Shall in eternity rejoice,
Where endless comforts flow.

LONGING FOR CHRIST. 8s.

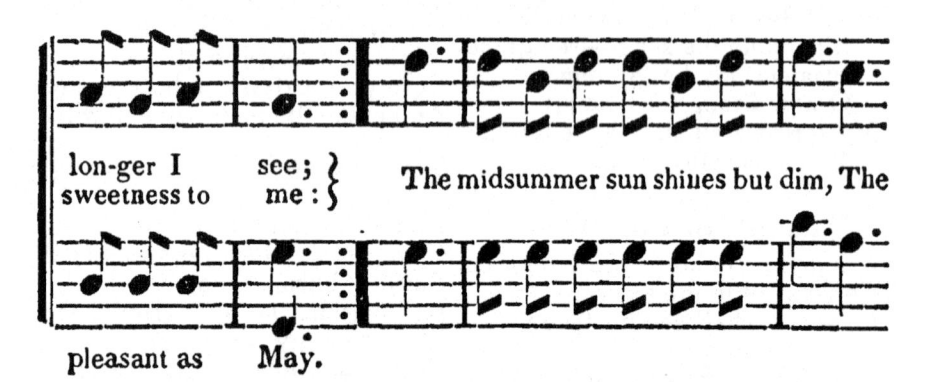

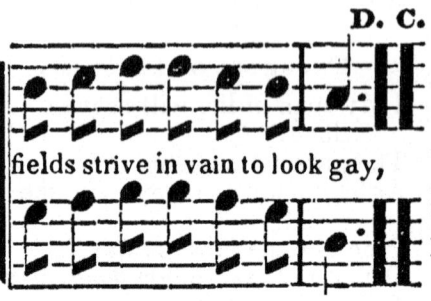

1. How tedious and tasteless the hours, When Jesus no longer I see;
Sweet prospects, sweet birds, and sweet flow'rs, Have all lost their sweetness to me:
The midsummer sun shines but dim, The fields strive in vain to look gay;
But when I am happy in him, December's as pleasant as May.

2
His name yields the richest perfume
And sweeter than music his voice;
His presence disperses my gloom,
And makes all within me rejoice:
I should, were he always thus nigh,
Have nothing to wish or to fear;
No mortal so happy as I,
My summer would last all the year.

3
Content with beholding his face,
My all to his pleasure resign'd;
No changes of season or place
Would make any change in my mind:
While blessed with a sense of his love,
A palace a toy would appear;
And prisons would palaces prove,
If Jesus would dwell with me there.

4
Dear Lord, if indeed I am thine,
If thou art my sun and my song,
Say, why do I languish and pine?
And why are my winters so long?
O drive these dark clouds from my sky,
Thy soul cheering presence restore:
Or take me to thee up on high,
Where winter and clouds are no more.

Israel's Shepherd.

1 Thou Shepherd of Israel and mine,
The joy and desire of my heart,
For closer communion I pine,
I long to reside where thou art;
The pasture I languish to find,
Where all who their Shepherd obey
Are fed, on thy bosom reclin'd,
And screen'd from the heat of the day.

2 Ah! show me that happiest place,
The place of thy people's abode;
Where saints in an ecstacy gaze,
And hang on a crucify'd God:
Thy love for a sinner declare;
Thy passion and death on the tree;
My spirit to Calvary bear,
To suffer and triumph with thee.

3 'Tis there with the lambs of thy flock,
There only I covet to rest;
To lie at the foot of the rock,
Or rise to be hid in thy breast;
'Tis there I would always abide,
And never a moment depart:
Conceal'd in the cleft of thy side.
Eternally held in thy heart.

Thirsting for Holiness.

1 What now is my object and aim?
What now is my hope and desire?
To follow the heavenly Lamb,
And after his image aspire:
My hope is all centred in thee;
I trust to recover thy love:
On earth thy salvation to see,
And then to enjoy it above.

2 I thirst for a life giving God,
A God that on Calvary died:
A fountain of water and blood
That gush'd from Immanuel's side!
I gasp for the streams of thy love,
The spirit of rapture unknown;
And then to re-drink it above,
Eternally fresh from the throne.

Our Father's House.

1 Away with our sorrow and fear,
We soon shall recover our home;
The city of saints shall appear;
The day of eternity come.
From earth we shall quickly remove,
And mount to our native abode;
The house of our Father above,
The palace of angels and God.

2 Our mourning is all at an end,
When, rais'd by the life-giving Word,
We see the new city descend,
Adorn'd as a bride for her Lord·
The city so holy and clean,
No sorrow can breathe in the air;
No gloom of affliction or sin;
No shadow of evil is there!

3 By faith we already behold
That lovely Jerusalem here;
Her walls are of jasper and gold,
As crystal her buildings are clear;
Immovably founded in grace,
She stands, as she ever hath stood,
And brightly her Builder displays,
And flames with the glory of God

4 No need of the sun in that day,
Which never is follow'd by night,
Where Jesus's beauties display,
A pure and a permanent light;
The Lamb is their Light and their Sun,
And lo! by reflection they shine;
With Jesus ineffably one,
And bright in effulgence divine!

5 The saints in his presence receive
Their great and eternal reward;
In Jesus, in heaven they live;
They reign in the smile of their Lord!
The flame of angelical love
Is kindled at Jesus's face;
And all the enjoyment above
Consists in the rapturous gaze!

48. Oh for that tenderness of Heart. C. M. D.

1. O for that ten-der-ness of heart Which bows be-fore the Lord; Acknowledging how just thou art And trem-bling at thy word! O for those humble con-trite tears, Which from re-pen-tance flow,
That consciousness of guilt which fears, The long suspended blow.

2 And will the Lord thus condescend,
To visit dying worms!
Thus at the door shall mercy stand,
In all her winning forms.
Amazing grace! and can my heart
Unmoved and cold remain;
Has this hard rock no tender part,
Shall mercy plead in vain?

3 Savior, to me, in pity give
The sensible distress;
The pledge thou wilt, at last, receive,
And bid me die in peace:
Wilt from the dreadful day remove,
Before the evil come;
My spirit hide with saints above,
My body in the tomb.

Providence ever faithful.

1
When all thy mercies, O my God,
My rising soul surveys;
Transported with the view, I'm lost
In wonder, love, and praise!
O how can words with equal warmth
The gratitude declare,
That glows within my ravish'd heart?
But thou canst read it there!

2
To all my weak complaints and cries,
Thy mercy lent an ear;
Ere yet my feeble thoughts had learn'd
To form themselves in prayer.
Unnumbered comforts on my soul
Thy tender care bestow'd;
Before my infant heart conceiv'd
From whom those comforts flow'd.

3
When in the slippery paths of youth,
With heedless steps I ran;
Thine arm, unseen, convey'd me safe,
And led me up to man.
Through hidden dangers, toils, and deaths,
It gently clear'd my way;
And through the pleasing snares of vice,
More to be feared than they.

4
Through every period of my life
Thy goodness I'll pursue;
And after death, in distant worlds,
The pleasing theme renew.
Through all eternity to thee
A grateful song I'll raise;
But O! eternity's too short
To utter all thy praise.

Christian Union.

1 Our souls, by love together knit,
Cemented, mix'd in one, [voice;
One hope, one heart, one mind, one
'Tis heaven on earth begun:
Our hearts have often burn'd within,
And glow'd with sacred fire,
While Jesus spoke, and fed, and bless'd,
And fill'd the enlarged desire.

2 The little cloud increases still,
The heavens are big with rain,
We wait to catch the teeming shower,
And all its moisture drain:
A rill, a stream, a torrent flows
But pour a mighty flood;
O sweep the nations, shake the earth,
Till all proclaim thee God. [up,

3 And when thou makest thy jewels
And set's thy starry crown,
When all thy sparkling gems shall shine,
Proclaimed by thee thine own;
May we, a little band of love,
We, sinners, saved by grace,
From glory unto glory changed,
Behold thee face to face.

Unalloyed Delights.

1 O 'tis delight, without alloy,
Jesus, to hear thy name;
My spirit leaps with inward joy,
I feel the sacred flame.
My passions hold a pleasing reign,
When love inspires my breast,
Love, the divinest of the train,
The sovereign of the rest.

2 This is the grace must live and sing,
When faith and hope shall cease,
Must sound from every joyful string
Through the sweet groves of bliss.
Let life immortal seize my clay;
Let love refine my blood;
Her flames can bear my soul away,
Can bring me near my God.

3 Swift I ascend the heavenly place,
And hasten to my home,
I leap to meet thy kind embrace,
I come, O Lord, I come.
Sink down, ye separating hills,
Let sin and death remove;
'Tis love that drives my chariot wheels,
And death must yield to love.

[5]

50. SONNET. 8s & 4.

Arranged for this work.

1. When for e-ter-nal worlds we steer, And seas are calm, and skies are clear,
And faith in live-ly ex-er-cise, And dis-tant hills of Canaan rise,
The soul for joy then claps her wings, And loud her love-ly sonnet sings, Vain world adieu, Vain world adieu. And loud her love-ly son-net sings; Vain world a-dieu.

2 With cheerful hope her eyes explore
Each landmark on the distant shore;
The trees of life, the pastures green,
The golden streets, the crystal stream;
Again for joy she claps her wings,
And loud her lovely sonnet sings,
   Vain world adieu.

3 The nearer still she draws to land,
More eager all her powers expand;
With steady helm, and free bent sail,
Her anchor drops within the vail;
Again for joy she claps her wings,
And her celestial sonnet sings,
   Glory to God.

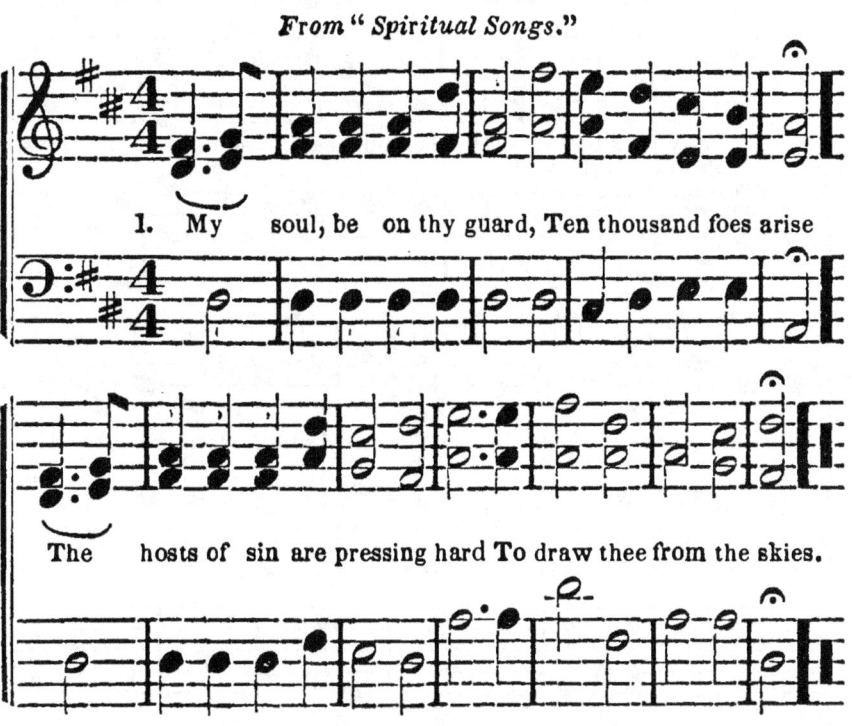

LABAN. S. M.
From " Spiritual Songs."

1. My soul, be on thy guard, Ten thousand foes arise
The hosts of sin are pressing hard To draw thee from the skies.

2 Oh watch, and fight, and pray;
  The battle ne'er give o'er;
Renew it boldly every day,
  And help divine implore.

3 Ne'er think the victory won,
  Nor lay thine armor down;
Thy arduous work will not be done
  Till thou obtain thy crown.

4 Fight on, my soul, till death
  Shall bring thee to thy God;
He'll take thee, at thy parting (breath,
  Up to his blest abode.

1 Soldiers of Christ, arise,
  And put your armor on,
Strong in the strength which God supplies
  Through his eternal Son;

2 Strong in the Lord of Hosts,
  And in his mighty power,
Who in the strength of Jesus trusts,
  Is more than conqueror.

3 Stand then in his great might,
  With all his strength endu'd;
But take, to arm you for the fight,
  The panoply of God.

52. THE GLORIOUS TREASURE. P. M.

Arranged and Harmonized for this work.

1. Re-li-gion is a glo-ri-ous treasure, The pur-chase of a Sav-ior's blood; It calms our fears, it soothes our sorrows, It smooths our way o'er life's rough sea, 'Tis mixed with goodness, meek, hum-ble pa-tience, This heavenly por-tion mine shall be.
It fills the mind with con-so-la-tion, It lifts the heart to things a-bove,

2 How vain, how fleeting, how tran-sitory!
This world with all its pomp and [show,
Its vain delights and delusive pleasures,
I gladly leave them all below:
But grace and glory shall be my story,
While I in Jesus such beauties see;
While endless ages are onward rolling
This heavenly portion mine shall be.

3 This earthly house shall be dissolv'd
And mortal life will soon be o'er—
All earthly cares and earthly sorrows
Shall pain my heart and eyes no more;
Yet 'pure religion' remains forever,
And strengthened my glad heart shall be;
While endless ages are onward rolling,
This heavenly portion mine shall be.

GIVE ME JESUS. 53

Arranged for this work.

While I'm happy, hear me cry, While I'm happy, hear me cry, While I'm happy, hear me cry, Give me Jesus, give me

Ad lib.

Je-sus, give me Je-sus, You may have all the world, give me Je-sus.

While I'm happy, hear me cry, &c.
Give me Jesus, &c.
While I'm singing, hear me cry, &c.
Give me Jesus, &c.
While I'm dying, hear me cry, &c.
Give me Jesus, &c.
While I'm rising, hear me cry, &c.
Give me Jesus, &c.
When I'm reigning, hear me sing, &c.
I have Jesus, &c.
And forever I will sing, &c.
I have Jesus, &c.

[5*]

54. Jesus, lover of my soul. 7s.

1. Jesus, lover of my soul, Let me to thy bosom fly,
While the nearer waters roll, While the tempest still is high;
Hide me, O my Savior, hide, Till the storm of life is past.
Safe in-to the haven guide, O receive my soul at last.

2
Other refuge have I none,
 Hangs my helpless soul on thee,
Leave, ah! leave me not alone,
 Still support and comfort me!
All my trust on thee is stay'd,
 All my help from thee I bring,
Cover my defenceless head
 With the shadow of thy wing.
3
Thou, O Christ, art all I want;
 More than all in thee I find,
Raise the fall'n, cheer the faint,
 Heal the sick, and lead the blind.
Just and holy is thy name;
 I am all unrighteousness.
False, and full of sin I am,
 Thou art full of truth and grace.

Lord, we seek thee.
1
Lord, we come before thee now,
At thy feet we humbly bow;
O! do not our suit disdain;
Shall we seek thee, Lord, in vain?
Lord, on thee our souls depend;
In compassion now descend;
Fill our hearts with thy rich grace,
Tune our lips to sing thy praise.
2
In thine appointed way,
Now we seek thee, here we stay;
Lord we know not how to go,
Till a blessing thou bestow.
Send some message from thy word,
That may joy and peace afford;
Let thy spirit now impart
Full salvation to each heart.
3
Comfort those who weep and mourn,
Let the time of joy return;
Those that are cast down lift up,
Make them st   hope.
Grant that al   find,
Thee a gra   nd;
Heal the sick, the captive free;
Let us all rejoice in thee.

The Love Feast.
1
Come, and let us sweetly join,
Christ to praise in hymns divine!
Give we all with one accord,
Glory to our common Lord;
Hands, and hearts, and voices raise;
Sing as in the ancient days,
Antedate the joys above,
Celebrate the feast of love.
2
Strive we, in affection strive:
Let the purer flame revive;
Such as in the martyrs glow'd,
Dying champions for their God;
We like them may live and love;
Call'd we are their joys to prove;
Sav'd with them from future wrath;
Partners of like precious faith.
3
Sing we then in Jesus's name,
Now as yesterday the same;
One in every time and place,
Full for all of truth and grace;
We for Christ, our Master, stand,
Lights in a benighted land
We our dying Lord confess,
We are Jesus' witnesses.
4
Come, thou high and lofty Lord!
Lowly, meek, incarnate Word;
Humbly stoop to earth again
Come and visit abject man!
Jesus, dear expected guest,
Thou art bidden to the feast:
For thyself our hearts prepare;
Come, and sit, and banquet there!
5
Jesus, we thy promise claim:
We are met in thy great name;
In the midst do thou appear,
Manifest thy presence here!
Sanctify us, Lord, and bless!
Breathe thy Spirit, give thy peace;
Thou thyself within us move
Make our feast a feast of love.

56. THE JUDGMENT SCENE.

1. The judgment day is rolling on, The judgment day is rolling on. The Judgment day is roll-ing on, As fast as time can move.

Oh! there will be mourning, mourning, mourn-ing, mourning, Oh there will be mourning, At the judgment seat of Christ.

2 This congregation there may part,
There wives and husbands soon may part,
There friends and neighbors soon may May part to meet no more. [part,
Oh there will be mourning, &c.

3 Parents and children there may part
Brothers and sisters there may part,

Pastors and people there may part,
May part to meet no more.
O there will be mourning, &c.

4 The heirs of glory there will meet,
Saints and angels there will meet,
Th' blood-wash'd comp'ny there will
Will meet to part no more. (meet,
O there will be glory, &c.

Come let us anew. 57

NOTE.—*The late Bishop Emory, when a delegate to the British Conference in 1824, brought this tune on his return—it has been universally admired.*

1. Come let us a-new our journey pursue, Roll round with the year, Roll round with the year, And never stand still till the Master appear, And never stand still till the Master appear.

2. His adorable will let us gladly fulfil, And our talents improve, And our talents improve, By the patience of hope, and the labor of love, By the patience of hope, and the labor of love.

3 Our life as a dream, our time as a stream
    Glides swiftly away ;
And the fugitive moment refuses to stay.

4 The arrow is flown, the moment is gone;
    The millenial year
Rushes on to our view, and eternity's here.

5 O that each in the day of his coming may say,
    " I have fought my way through ;
I have finish'd the work thou didst give me to do !"

6 O that each from his Lord may receive the glad word,
    " Well and faithfully done !
Enter into my joy, and sit down on my throne "

58 O Fly Mourning Sinner. 11s.

1. O fly mourning sinner, saith Jesus to me, Thy guilt I will pardon, thy soul I will free; From the chains that have bound thee, My grace shall release, And thy stains I will wash, and thy sorrows shall cease.

2 Too long, guilty wanderer, too long hast thou been,
   In the broad road of ruin, in bondage to sin;
   Thee the world has allur'd, and enslav'd, and deceiv'd,
   While my counsel thou'st spurn'd, and my Spirit hast grieved.

3 Though countless thy sins, and though crimson thy guilt,
   Yet for crimes such as thine was my blood freely spilt;
   Come sinner, and prove me; come, mourner, and see
   The wounds that I bore, when I suffer'd for thee.

4 Thou doubd'st not my power—deny not my will;
   Come, needy, come, helpless, thy soul I will fill;
   My mercy is boundless; no sinner shall say,
   That he sued at my feet—but was driven away.   J. B. W

Delay not, O Sinner.

1 Delay not, delay not, O Sinner draw near!
   No price is demanded, the Savior is here,
   The waters of life are now flowing for thee
   Redemption is purchased, salvation is free.

2 Delay not, delay not, O sinner to come
   For mercy is heard not, 'mid shades of the tomb;
   Yet mercy still lingers, and calls thee to day,
   Her message unheeded, will soon pass away.

3 Delay not, delay not, no longer abuse
   His love and compassion; how can you refuse
   The fountain that's opened in Jesus, thy God;
   Oh wash and be cleansed in his saving blood

FEAR NOT LITTLE FLOCK.

1. Glo-ry to God that I have found, The pearl of my salvation;
I'm marching through Immanuel's ground, Up to my heavenly station;
And I'm resolved to travel on, And nev-er to for-sake him.
I'll always keep the narrow way, Till I do o-ver-take him.

2 Fear not, says Christ, ye little flock   Fight on, fight on, ye heirs of grace,
Heirs of immortal glory;   And tell the pleasing story,
For ye are built upon the rock,   I'm with my little flock always,
The kingdom lies before you.   I'll bring them home to glory.

LOVE DIVINE. 8s & 7s.

From "Spiritual Songs"

1. Love di-vine, all love ex-cell-ing, Joy of heaven to earth come down, Fix in us thy humble dwell-ing, All thy faith-ful mercies crown, Je-sus thou art all com-pas-sion, Pure, un-bound-ed love thou art, Vis-it

2. Breathe, O breathe thy loving spir-it, In-to ev-ery troubled breast! Let us all in thee in-her-it, Let us find that sec-ond rest, Take a-way our bent of sin-ning, Al-pha and O-me-ga be, End of

us with thy sal-va-tion, En-ter ev-ery trembling heart.
faith as its be-gin-ning, Set our hearts at lib-er-ty.

3 Come, Almighty to deliver,
Let us all thy grace receive,
Suddenly return, and never,
Never more thy temples leave!
Thee we would be always blessing,
Serve thee as thy hosts above,
Pray, and praise thee without ceasing,
Glory in thy perfect love.

4 Finish then, thy new creation,
Pure and spotless let us be;
Let us see thy great salvation,
Perfectly restored in thee!
Changed from glory into glory,
Till in heaven we take our place,
Till we cast our crowns before thee
Lost in wonder, love, and praise!
WESLEY.

Sanctification.

1 Ye who know your sins forgiven,
And are happy in the Lord,
Have you read that gracious promise,
Which is left upon record;
I will sprinkle you with water,
I will cleanse you from all sin
Sanctify and make you holy,
I will dwell and reign within.

2 Tho' you have much peace and comfort,
Greater things you yet may find,
Freedom from unholy tempers,
Freedom from the carnal mind.
To procure your perfect freedom,
Jesus suffer'd, groan'd, and died,
On the cross the healing fountain,
Gushed from his wounded side.

3 If you have obtained this treasure
Search and you shall surely find
All the christian marks and graces,
Planted, growing in your mind.
Perfect faith, and perfect patience,
Perfect lowliness, and then
Perfect hope, and perfect meekness,
Perfect love for God and man.

4 But be sure to gain the witness,
Which abides both day and night;
This your God has plainly promis'd,
This is like a stream of light.
While you keep the blessed witness
All is clear and calm within,
God himself assures you by it
That your heart is cleansed from sin.

5 Be as holy and as happy,
And as useful here below,
As it is your Father's pleasure,
Jesus, only Jesus know.
Spread, O spread the holy fire,
Tell, O tell what God has done,
Till the nations are conformed
To the image of his Son.

6 Wake up brother, wake up sister,
Seek, O seek this holy state;
None but holy ones can enter
'Thro' the pure celestial gate.
Can you bear the tho't of losing
All the joys that are above?
No, my brother, no, my sister,
God will perfect you in love.

[6]

62. LENOX. H. M.

1. Arise, my soul, arise, Shake off thy guilty fears, The bleeding Sacrifice In my behalf appears; Before the throne my Surety stands, Before the throne my Surety stands, Before the throne my Surety stands, My name is written on his hands.

Faith in Christ.

2 He ever lives above,
  For me to intercede ;
His all-redeeming love,
  His precious blood to plead ;
His blood aton'd for all our race,
And sprinkles now the throne of grace.

3 Five bleeding wounds he bears,
  Receiv'd on Calvary ;
They pour effectual prayers,
  They strongly speak for me ;
Forgive him, O forgive, they cry,
Nor let that ransom'd sinner die !

4 The Father hears him pray,
  His dear anointed One ;
He cannot turn away
  The presence of his Son ;
His Spirit answers to the blood,
And tells me I am born of God.

5 My God is reconcil'd,
  His pard'ning voice I hear ;
He owns me for his child,
  I can no longer fear ;
With confidence I now draw nigh,
And Father, Abba Father, cry.

Excellence of Christ.

1 Let earth and heaven agree,
  Angels and men be join'd
To celebrate with me
  The Savior of mankind ;
T'adore the all-atoning Lamb,
And bless the sound of Jesus' name.

2 Jesus ! transporting sound !
  The joy of earth and heaven ;
No other help is found,
  No other name is given,
By which we can salvation have ;
But Jesus came the world to save.

3 Jesus ! harmonious name !
  It charms the hosts above ;
They evermore proclaim,
  And wonder at his love !
'Tis all their happiness to gaze,
'Tis heaven to see our Jesus' face.

4 His name the sinner hears,
  And is from sin set free ;
'Tis music in his ears ;
  'Tis life and victory ;
New songs do now his lips employ,
And dances his glad heart for joy.

The Year of Jubilee.

1 Blow ye the trumpet, blow,
  The gladly solemn sound ;
Let all the nations know,
  To earth's remotest bound ;
The year of Jubilee is come ;
Return, ye ransom'd sinners, home.

2 Jesus, our great High Priest,
  Hath full atonement made ;
Ye weary spirits, rest,
  Ye mournful souls, be glad ;
The year of Jubilee is come ;
Return, ye ransom'd sinners, home.

3 Extol the Lamb of God,
  The all-atoning Lamb ;
Redemption in his blood
  Throughout the world proclaim ;
The year of Jubilee is come ;
Return, ye ransom'd sinners, home.

4 Ye who have sold for nought
  Your heritage above,
Shall have it back unbought,
  The gift of Jesus' love ;
The year of Jubilee is come ;
Return, ye ransom'd sinners, home.

5 The gospel trumpet hear,
  The news of heavenly grace
And, sav'd from earth, appear
  Before your Savior's face ;
The year of Jubilee is come ;
Return, ye ransom'd sinners, home.

Freedom from Sin.

1 Ye ransom'd sinners, hear,
  The prisoners of the Lord ;
And wait till Christ appear,
  According to his word ;
Rejoice in hope, rejoice with me,
We shall from all our sins be free.

2 Let others hug their chains,
  For sin and Satan plead,
And say, from sin's remains
  They never can be free ;
Rejoice in hope, rejoice with me,
We shall from all our sins be free.

3 In God we put our trust ;
  If we our sins confess,
Faithful is he, and just,
  From all unrighteousness
To cleanse us all, both you and me ;
We shall from all our sins be free.

64. Saw ye my Savior!

Very Slow.

1. Saw ye my Savior! Saw ye my Savior! Saw ye my Savior God! O he died on Cal-va-ry, To atone for you and me, And to purchase our pardon with blood.

2. He was extended, he was extended,
Painfully nail'd to the cross;
There he bowed his head and died,
There my Lord was crucified,
To atone for a world that was lost.

3
Jesus hung bleeding, Jesus hung bleeding,
Three dreadful hours in pain;
And the solid rocks were rent,
Through creation's vast extent,
When the Jews crucified the Lamb.

4
Darkness prevail'd, Darkness prevailed,
Darkness prevail'd o'er the land;
And the sun refused to shine,
While his Majesty divine
Was derided, insulted and slain.

5
When it was finish'd, when it was finish'd,
And the atonement was made,
He was taken by the great,
And embalmed in spices sweet,
And was in a new sepulchre laid.

6
Hail, mighty Savior, hail, mighty Savior,
Prince and the Author of peace,
Soon he burst the bands of death,
And triumphant, from the earth,
He ascended to mansions of bliss.

7
There interceding, there interceding,
Pleading that sinners may live,
Crying, "See my hands and side,
Father, I was crucified
To redeem them, I pray thee forgive.

8
"I will forgive them, I will forgive them
When they repent and believe;
Let them now return to thee,
And be reconcil'd to me,
And salvation they all shall receive."

When we all meet in Heaven. P. M. 65

1. The wond'rous love of Jesus! From doubts and fears he frees us, With pitying eyes he sees us, While trav'ling here below, *Till we all meet in heaven, Till we all meet in heaven; There we shall meet, There we shall meet to part no more.*

2. And there we shall forever, Drink of that flowing river, And ever, ever, ever, Surround the throne above. *When we all meet in heaven, When we all meet in heaven, There we shall meet, There we shall meet to part no more.*

3 There in the blooming garden
Of Eden gained by pardon,—
Upon the banks of Jordan,
We'll worship then the Lamb.
When we all meet in heaven, &c.

4 We'll sing the song of Moses,
While Jesus sweet composes,
A song that never closes,
Of praises to his name.
When we all meet in heaven, &c.

66. FREE SALVATION. P. M.

Arranged for this work.

1. Man at his first cre-a-tion, In Eden God did place, The public head and Father, Of all the human race; But by the subtle serpent, Beguil'd he was and fell, And by his dis-o-be-di-ence, Was doomed to death and hell.

2 While in this situation,
　A promise there was made,
The offspring of the woman
　Should bruise the serpent's head.
Against the power of Satan,
　That man might only feel,
The malice of the serpent,
　Enraging at his heel.

3 Now at the time appointed,
　Jesus unveiled his face,
Assumed our human nature,
　And suffered in our place;
He suffered on mount Calvary,
　And ransomed all for me,
The law demands attention,
　To pay the penalty.

4 They laid him in a sepulchre
　It being near at hand,
The grave now could not hold him,
　Nor death's cold iron band.
He burst them all asunder,
　And pull'd their kingdoms down,
He's overcome his enemies,
　And wears a starry crown.

5 Now at the resurrection
　To Mary he appeared,
Saying, tell to my disciples,
　What you have seen and heard,
Go tell them I am risen,
　My suffering time is o'er,
I'm going to my Father
　To reign forevermore.

6 He came to his disciples,
　And found them all alone,
And gave them their commission
　To make his gospel known;
Go preach it to all nations,
　Baptize them in my name,
Beginning at Jerusalem,
　'Twas there I suffered shame.

7 Go preach it to all nations,
　That they may hear and know,
Go publish free salvation,
　That men to heaven may go;
In every sore temptation,
　You succor I will send,
And lo! I will be with you
　Until the world shall end.

FIDELITY. P. M.

Oh brethren be faithful, Oh brethren be faithful, O brethren be faith-ful, faithful, faithful Till we all arrive at home.

Oh sisters be faithful, &c.
Till we all arrive at home.

There shall we see Jesus, &c.
When we all arrive at home.

Then we will shout glory, &c.
When we all arrive at home.

There'll be no more parting, &c.
When we all arrive at home.

STAR OF BETHLEHEM. L. M. D.

1. When marshalled on the night-ly plain, A glitt'ring host be-stud the sky; One star a-lone of all the train, Can fix the sinner's wand'-ring eye. But one a-lone the Sa-vior speaks, It is the star of Beth-le-hem. Hark

Hark! to God the chorus breaks, From ev'ry host, from ev'-ry gem;

WESLEYAN PSALMIST.   69

2 Once on the raging seas I rode ;
The storm was loud, the night was
    dark,   [blowed,
The ocean yawned, and rudely
The wind that tossed my founder-
    ing bark.
Deep horror then my vitals froze ;
Death struck, I ceased the tide to
When suddenly a star arose, [stem:
It was the star of Bethlehem.

3 It was my guide, my light, my all;
It bade my dark forebodings cease;
And through the storm and dan-
    ger's thrall,
It led me to the port of peace.
Now safely moor'd, my perils
    o'er,
I'll sing, first in night's diadem,
Forever, and forever more,
The star, the star of Bethlehem.

Sinner's Come.

1 Come sinners, to the Gospel feast
Let every soul be Jesus' guest ;
Ye need not one be left behind
For God hath bidden all mankind.
Sent by my Lord, on you I call ;
The invitation is to all :   [thou !
Come, all the world! come, sinner,
All things in Christ are ready now.

2 Come, all ye souls by sin op-
    press'd,
Ye restless wand'rers after rest ;
Ye poor, and maim'd, and halt,
    and blind,
In Christ a hearty welcome find.
My message as from God receive ;
Ye all may come to Christ and live:
O let his love your hearts constrain,
Nor suffer him to die in vain !

3 His love is mighty to compel ;
His conqu'ring love consent to feel:
Yield to his love's resistless power,
And fight against your God no
    more.
See him set forth before your eyes,
That precious, bleeding sacrifice !
His offer'd benefits embrace,
And freely now be sav'd by grace!

Ho, every one that thirsts.

1 Ho! every one that thirsts, draw
    nigh ;
'Tis God invites the fallen race ;
Mercy and free salvation buy,
Buy wine, and milk, and Gospel
    grace.
Come to the living waters, come !
Sinners, obey your Maker's call ;
" Return, ye weary wand'rers,
    home,
And find my grace is free for all."

2 See from the rock a fountain rise;
For you in healing streams it rolls;
Money ye need not bring, nor price,
Ye lab'ring, burden'd, sin sick souls
Nothing ye in exchange shall give,
Leave all you have, and are,
    behind ;
Frankly the gift of God receive,
Pardon and peace in Jesus find.

3 " Why seek ye that which is not
    bread,
Nor can your hungry souls sustain?
On ashes, husks, and air ye feed ;
Ye spend your little all in vain.
In search of empty joys below,
Ye toil with unavailing strife :
Whither, ah! whither would ye go?
I have the words of endless life.

The Sabbath.

1 Sweet is the work, my God, my
    King,   [and sing,
To praise thy name, give thanks
To show thy love by morning light,
And talk of all thy truth by night.
Sweet is the day of sacred rest,
No mortal cares shall seize my
    breast,
O may my heart in tune be found,
Like David's harp of solemn sound!

2 When grace has purified my heart,
Then I shall share a glorious part :
And fresh supplies of joy are shed,
Like holy oil to cheer my head.
Then shall I see and hear, and know
All I desir'd or wish'd below ;
And every hour find sweet employ,
In that eternal world of joy.

70. Jesus says he will be with us. L. M.

Arranged for this work.

1. Chil-dren of God re-nounce your fears; } Je-sus
   Lo! Je-sus for your help ap-pears.   }

2. He loud-ly speaks, as he draws nigh,   } Je-sus
   "Be not a-fraid, for *it is I.*"   }

says he will be with us to the end, For he has been with us, and he

still is with us, And he's promised to be with us to the end.

3 When in the awful tempest tost, *Jesus says,* &c.
   You feel your strength and courage lost, *Jesus says,* &c.
    For he, &c.

4 When mighty waves roll o'er your head, *Jesus says,* &c.
   Your Lord is near, be not afraid, *Jesus says,* &c.
    For he, &c.

5 When fierce disease attacks your frame, *Jesus says,* &c.
   Your Savior's love is still the same, *Jesus says,* &c.
    For he, &c.

6 In death's dark shade you need not fear, *Jesus says,* &c.
   For Jesus will be with you there, *Jesus says,* &c.
    For he, &c.

THE LORD WILL PROVIDE. 10s & 11s.

Arranged for this work.

1. Tho' trou-bles as-sail, and dangers affright, Though friends should all fail, and foes all unite, Yet one thing secures us, what-ever betide, The promise assures us, The Lord will provide, The Lord will provide.

2 When Satan appears to stop up our path,
And fills us with fears, we triumph by faith;
He cannot take from us, (tho' oft he has tried,)
The heart-cheering promise, The Lord will provide.

3 No strength of our own, nor goodness we claim;
Our trust is all thrown on Jesus's name;
In this our strong tower for safety we hide;
The Lord is our power, The Lord will provide.

4 When life sinks apace, and death heaves in view
The word of his grace shall comfort us through;
Not fearing or doubting, with Christ on our side,
We hope to die shouting, The Lord will provide

72 EDEN OF LOVE.

By John J. Hicks. *Christian Lyre.*

1. How sweet to reflect on those joys that await me, In yon blissful region, the haven of rest, Where glorified spirits with welcome shall greet me, And lead me to mansions prepared for the blest; En-cir-cled in light And with glo-ry en-shroud-ed, My

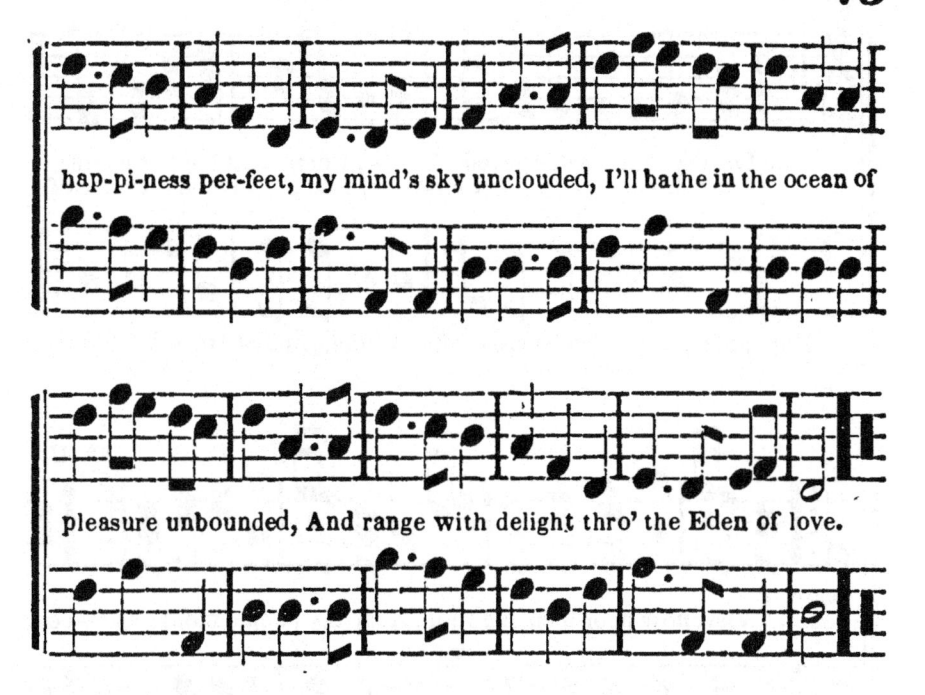

1 How sweet to reflect on those joys that await me,
  In yon blissful region, the haven of rest;
 Where glorified spirits with welcome shall meet me,
  And lead me to mansions prepared for the blest;
 Encircled in light, and with glory enshrouded,
 My happiness perfect, my mind's sky unclouded,
 I'll bathe in the ocean of pleasure unbounded,
  And range with delight through the Eden of Love.

2 While angelic legions, with harps tuned celestial,
  Harmoniously join in the concert of praise,
 The saints, as they flock from the regions terrestrial,
  In loud hallelujahs their voices shall raise;
 Then songs to the Lamb shall re-echo through heaven,
 My soul will respond, to Immanuel be given
 All glory, all honor, all might and dominion,
  Who brought us through grace to the Eden of Love.

3 Then hail, blessed state! Hail ye songsters of glory!
  Ye harpers of bliss, soon I'll meet you above!
 And join your full choir in rehearsing the story,
  "Salvation from sorrow, through Jesus's love."
 Though prisoned in earth, yet by anticipation,
 Already my soul feels a sweet prelibation,
 Of joys that await me, when freed from probation;
  My heart's now in heaven, the Eden of Love!

[7]

THE GOOD SHEPHERD.

1. Let thy kingdom, blessed Savior, Come, and bid our jarring cease.
Come, O come, and reign for-ev-er, God of love and prince of peace.
Day and night thy lambs are crying, Come, good Shepherd, feed thy sheep.
Visit now poor bleeding Zion, Hear thy people mourn and weep.

2 Lord, in us there is no merit,
  We were sinners in our youth,
Guide us, Lord, by thy good Spirit,
  Which shall teach us all the truth.
On thy gospel word we'll venture,
  Till in death's cold arms we sleep,
Love our Lord, and Christ our Savior,
  O! good Shepherd, feed thy sheep.

3 Come, good Lord, with courage arm us,
  Persecution rages here,—
Nothing, Lord, we know can harm us,
  While our Shepherd is so near.
Glory, glory be to Jesus,
  At his name our hearts do leap;
He both comforts us and frees us,
  The good Shepherd feeds his sheep.

4 Hear the Prince of our salvation,
  Saying, "Fear not, little flock;
I myself am your Foundation,
  You are built upon this Rock;
Shun the paths of vice and folly,
  Scale the mount, although its steep,
Look to me, and be ye holy,
  I delight to feed my sheep."

5 Christ alone, whose merit saves us,
  Taught by him, we'll own his name,
Sweetest of all names is Jesus!
  How it doth our souls inflame.
Glory, glory, glory, glory,
  Give him glory, he will keep,
He will clear our way before us,
  The good Shepherd feeds his sheep.

Come, ye sinners. 6s & 7s.

NOTE.—*This is a popular tune and hymn to sing when inviting sinners forward for prayers.*

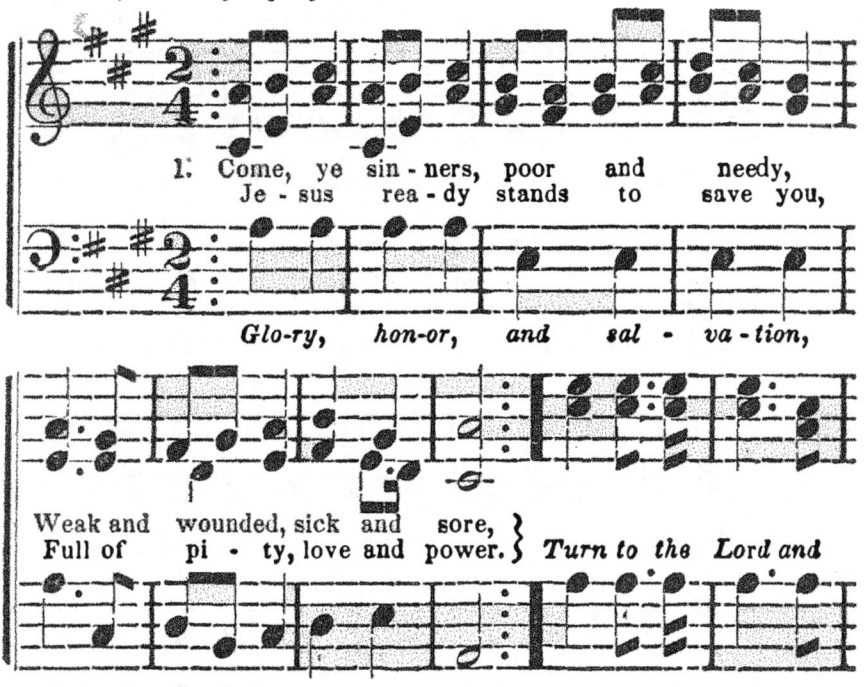

1. Come, ye sinners, poor and needy,
Jesus ready stands to save you,
Glory, honor, and salvation,
Weak and wounded, sick and sore,
Full of pity, love and power.
Turn to the Lord and seek salvation,
Sound the praise of his dear name;
Christ the Lord is come to reign.

2 Now, ye needy, come and welcome,
God's free bounty glorify;
True belief and true repentance,
Every grace that brings you nigh,
  Turn to the Lord, &c.

3 Let not conscience make you linger,
Nor of fitness fondly dream;
All the fitness he requireth
Is to feel your need of him;
  Turn to the Lord, &c.

4 Come, ye weary, heavy laden,
Bruis'd and mangled by the fall,
If you tarry till you're better,
You will never come at all;
  Turn to the Lord, &c.

5 Agonizing in the garden,
Lo! your Maker prostrate lies!
On the bloody tree, behold him!
Hear him cry before he dies,
  Turn to the Lord, &c.

76. THE PEARL OF GREAT PRICE.

Words by Rev. S. Hoyt.

1. The pearl that worldlings covet, is not the pearl for me, Its beauty fades as quickly, As sun-shine on the sea; But there's a pearl sought by the wise, It's call'd the pearl of greatest price: Though few its value see, O that's the pearl for humble love, For-ev-er bright 'twill be. O, that's the crown for

2. The crown that decks the monarch, is not the crown for me, It dazzles but a moment, Its brightness soon will flee; But there's a crown prepared above, For all who walk in

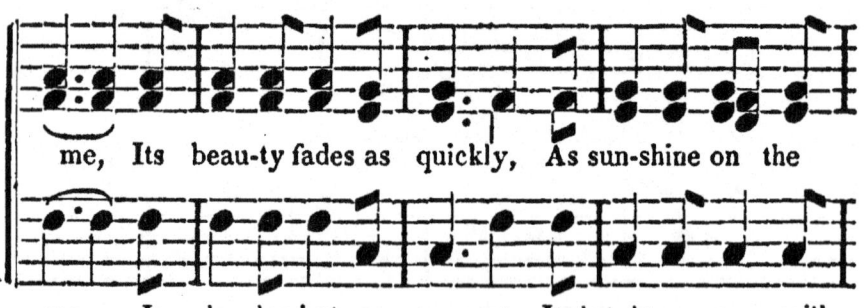

WESLEYAN PSALMIST. 77

me, O that's the pearl for me, O that's the pearl for me.

me, O, that's the crown for me, O, that's the crown for me!

3 The road that many travel,
  Is not the road for me :
It leads to death and sorrow,
  In it I would not be. [God,
But there's a road that leads to
  It's marked by Christ's most
    precious blood :
  The passage here is free.
  O, that's the road for me, &c.

4 The hope that sinners cherish
  Is not the hope for me ;
Most surely will they perish,
  Unless from sin made free.
But there's a hope which rests in
  God, [word
And leads the soul to keep his
  And sinful pleasures flee.
  O, that's the hope for me, &c.

Sinner can you hate the Savior?

Slow.

1. Now the Sav-ior stands and plead-ing, At the
Now in heaven he's in-ter-ce-ding, Un-der-
Once he died for your be--hav-ior, Now he

sin-ner's bolt-ed heart.
tak-ing sin-ner's part. *Sin-ner can you hate the Sav-ior?*
calls you to his arms.
D. C.

Can you thrust him from your arms.

2 Jesus stands, oh, how amazing,
Stands and knocks at ev'ry door ;
In his hands ten thousand blessings,
Proffer'd to the wretched poor, &c.

3 See him bleeding, dying rising,
To prepare you heavenly rest ;
Listen, while he kindly calls you,
Hear, and be forever blest, &c.

4 Now he has not come to judgment,
To condemn your wretched race ;
But to ransom ruined sinners,
And display unbounded grace, &c.

5 Will you plunge in endless dark-
There to bear eternal pain; [ness,
Or to realms of glorious brightness
Rise, and with him ever reign, &c.

[7*]

78 Oh for a closer walk with God. C. M.

1. O for a closer walk with God, A calm and heavenly frame;
A light to shine up-on the road That leads me to the Lamb.
Where is the bless-ed-ness I knew, When first I saw the Lord? Where is the soul-refreshing view Of Jesus and his word?

2 What peaceful hours I once en-joy'd,
How sweet their memory still!
But they have left an aching void
The world can never fill.
Return, O holy Dove, return,
Sweet messenger of rest!
I hate the sins that made thee mourn,
And drove me from thy breast.

3 The dearest idol I have known,
Whate'er that idol be,
Help me to tear it from thy throne,
And worship only thee.
So shall my walk be close with God,
Calm and serene my frame;
So purer light shall mark the road
That leads me to the Lamb.

WESLEYAN PSALMIST. 79

Babel's Streams.

1 Oh no, we cannot sing the songs,
Made for Jehovah's praise;
Our sorrowing harps refuse their strings,
To Zion's gladsome strains.
They bid us be in mirthful mood,
And dry these tears so sad;
But Judah's hearths are desolate,
And how can we be glad?

2 Silent our harps o'er Babel's streams
Are hung on willows wet;
And Zion we no more shall see;
But we can ne'er forget.
Jerusalem, thy banish'd ones,
Prove anguish and regret;
But heaven's own curse shall rest on them,
If thee they e'er forget.

The Faithful Friend.

1 O thou who driest the mourner's tear,
How dark this world would be,
If, pierced by sins and sorrows here,
We could not fly to thee!
The friends who in our sunshine live,
When winter comes, are flown;
And he who has but tears to give,
Must weep those tears alone.

2 Oh! who could bear life's stormy doom,
Did not thy wing of love
Come brightly wafting through the gloom,
Our peace-branch from above.
Then sorrow touched by thee, grows bright,
With more than rapture's ray:
As darkness shows us worlds of light,
We never saw by day.

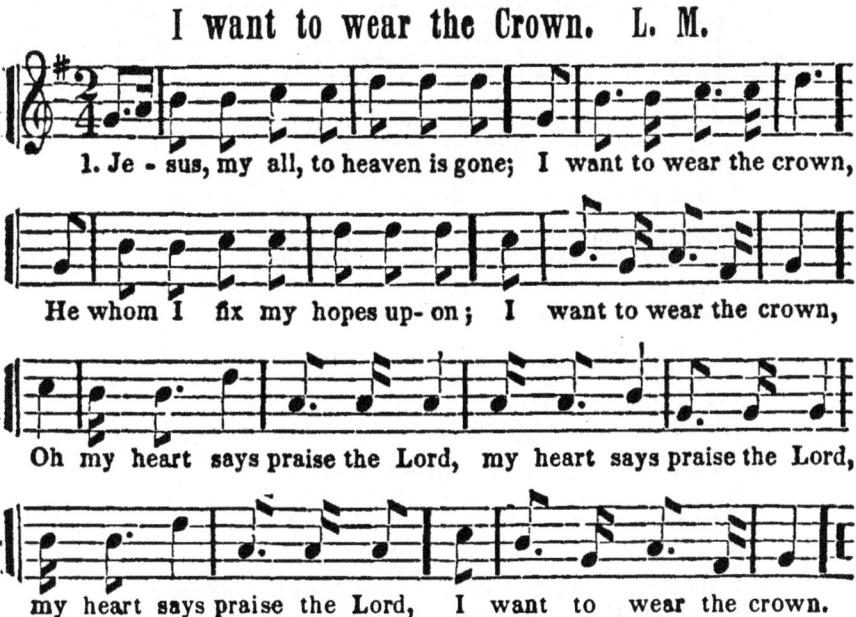

I want to wear the Crown. L. M.

1. Je-sus, my all, to heaven is gone; I want to wear the crown,
He whom I fix my hopes up-on; I want to wear the crown,
Oh my heart says praise the Lord, my heart says praise the Lord,
my heart says praise the Lord, I want to wear the crown.

2 The way the holy prophets went,
  I want to wear the crown,
The road that leads from banishment;
  I want to wear the crown,
Oh my heart says, &c.

3 His track I see, and I'll pursue,
  I want to wear the crown,
The narrow way, till him I view,
  I want to wear the crown,
Oh my heart says, &c.

4 The King's highway of holiness,
  I want to wear the crown,
I'll go, for all his paths are peace.
  I want to wear the crown,
Oh my heart says, &c.

5 Lo! glad I come, and thou, blest Lamb,
  I want to wear the crown,
Shalt take me to thee whose I am;
  I want to wear the crown,
Oh my heart says, &c.

80. Gethsemane; or, Christ in the Garden. P. M.

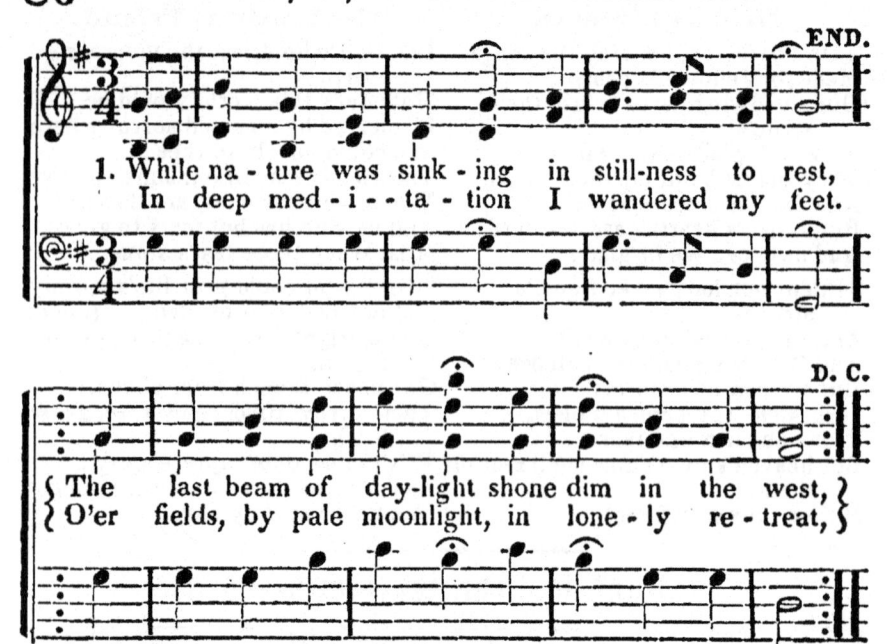

1. While nature was sinking in stillness to rest,
In deep meditation I wandered my feet.
The last beam of daylight shone dim in the west,
O'er fields, by pale moonlight, in lonely retreat,

2 While passing a garden I paused to hear,
A voice faint and plaintive, from one that was there;
The voice of the suff'rer affected my heart,
While pleading in anguish the poor sinner's part.

3 I listen'd a moment, then turn'd me to see
What man of compassion this stranger might be!
I saw him, low, kneeling, upon the cold ground,
The loveliest BEING that ever was found.

4 So deep were his sorrows, so fervent his prayers,
That down o'er his bosom roll'd sweat, blood, and tears!
I wept to behold him!—I ask'd him his name,
He answered,—" 'Tis JESUS! from heaven I came!

5 I am thy Redeemer! For thee I must die;
The cup is most bitter, but cannot pass by!
Thy sins, like a mountain, are laid upon me;
And all this deep anguish I suffer for thee."

6 How sweet was that moment he bade me rejoice!
His smile, O how pleasant! How cheering his voice!
I flew from the garden to spread it abroad,
I shouted Salvation! and Glory to God!

7 I'm now on my journey to mansions above;
My soul's full of glory, of light, peace and love!
I think of the garden, the prayers, and the tears,
Of that loving Stranger, who banished my fears!

8 The day of bright glory is rolling around,
When Gabriel descending—the trumpet shall sound;
My soul then in raptures of glory shall rise
To gaze on the Stranger with unclouded eyes.

NORTHFIELD. C. M.

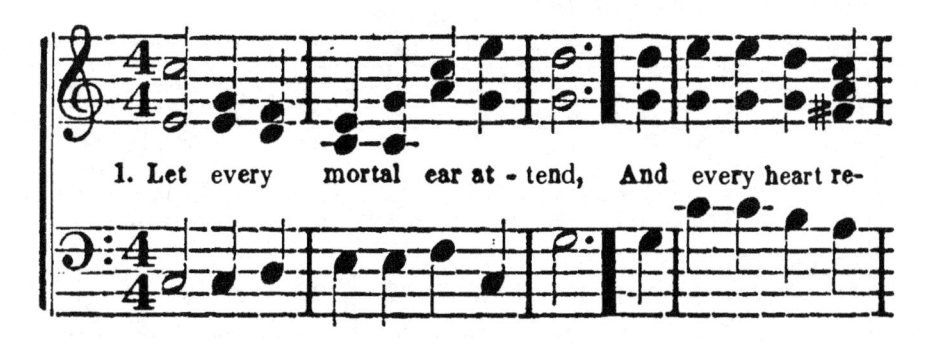

1. Let every mortal ear attend, And every heart rejoice; The trumpet of the Gospel sounds With an inviting voice, With an inviting voice.

2 Ho! all ye hungry, starving souls,
   That feed upon the wind,
And vainly strive with earthly toys,
   To fill an empty mind;

3 Eternal Wisdom hath prepar'd
   A soul-reviving feast,
And bids your longing appetites
   The rich provision taste.

4 Ho! ye that pant for living streams,
   And pine away and die,
Here you may quench your raging thirst
   With springs that never dry.

5 The happy gates of Gospel grace,
   Stand open night and day;
Lord, we are come to seek supplies
   And drive our wants away.

82. What glorious tidings. C. M. Double.

NOTE.—*The first Hymn in the Methodist Hymn Book is also a proper one to be sung with this tune.*

1. What glorious tidings do I hear, From my Redeemer's tongue! I can no longer silence bear; I'll break into a song, The blind receive their sight with joy, The lame can walk abroad, The dumb their loosened tongues employ, The deaf can hear the word.

2. The dead are raised to life anew, By renovating grace; The glorious gospel's preached to you, The poor of Adam's race; O wondrous type of things divine, When Christ displays his love, To raise from wo the sinking mind, To reign in realms above.

O land of rest, for thee I sigh. C. M. 83

Arranged for this work.

1. O land of rest, for thee I sigh, When will the moment come, When I shall lay my armor by, And dwell with Christ at home.

And dwell with Christ at home. When I shall lay my armor by, And dwell with Christ at home.

2
No tranquil joys on earth I know;
No peaceful, sheltering dome;
This world's a wilderness of wo;
This world is not my home.

3
To Jesus Christ I sought for rest,
He bade me cease to roam;
And fly for succor to his breast,
And he'd conduct me home.

4 When, by afflictions sharply tried,
I viewed the gaping tomb.
Although I dread death's chilling flood,
Yet still I sighed for home.

5 Weary of wandering round and round
This vale of sin and gloom, [
I long to leave the unhallowed ground,
And dwell with Christ at home.

Christ always new.

1 Since man by sin has lost his God,
He seeks creation through,
And vainly strives for solid bliss,
In trying something new.

2 Could I but call all Europe mine,
The Indies and Peru,
My soul would feel an aching void,
And still want something new.

3 But when we know the Savior's love,
All good in him we view:
The soul forsakes its vain delights,
In Christ find all things new.

4 The joy the dear Redeemer gives
Will bear us safely through,
Nor need we ever change again,
For Christ is always new.

84 THE BELOVED OF ZION. 11s & 8s.

Note.—*The late Doctor Fisk was particularly fond of this tune, and in the prayer meeting would frequently break forth alone in its strains.*

1. O thou in whose presence my soul takes delight, On whom in af-flic-tion I call; My comfort by day, and my song in the night, My hope, my sal-vation, my all.

2
O why should I wander an alien from thee;
  Or cry in the desert for bread;
Thy foes will rejoice when my sorrows they see,
  And smile at the tears I have shed.

3
Ye daughters of Zion, declare, have you seen,
  The Star that on Israel shone:
Say, if in your tents my Beloved has been,
  And where with his flock he has gone?

4
His voice as the sound of the dulcimer sweet,
　Is heard through the shadow of death,
The cedars of Lebanon bow at his feet,
　The air is perfumed with his breath.

5
His lips as a fountain of righteousness flow,
　To water the gardens of grace;
From which their salvation the Gentiles shall known
　And bask in the smiles of his face.

6
He looks, and ten thousand of angels rejoice,
　And myriads wait for his word;
He speaks, and eternity filled with his voice,
　Re-echoes the praise of the Lord.

LOVEST THOU ME! 7s

1. Hark, my soul, it is the Lord! 'Tis thy Savior, hear his word! Jesus speaks, he speaks to thee, 'Say, poor sinner, lovest thou me?'

2. "I deliver'd thee when bound, And when bleeding, heal'd thy wound, Sought thee wand'ring, set thee right, Turn'd thy darkness into light.

3 " Can a mother's tender care
Cease towards the child she bare?
Yes, she may forgetful be,
Yet I will remember thee.

4 " Mine is an unchanging love,
Higher than the heights above,
Deeper than the depths beneath,
Free and faithful, strong as death.

5 " Thou shalt see my glory soon,
When the work of faith is done,—
Partner of my throne shalt be:
Say, poor sinner, lovest thou me?"

6 Lord, it is my chief complaint
That my love is still so faint,
Yet I love thee, and adore:
O for grace to love thee more!

Jesus; or, The poor way-faring man.

1. A poor wayfaring man of grief Hath often crossed me on my way,
Who sued so humbly for re-lief, That I could never answer nay;
I had no pow'r to ask his name, Whither he went or whence he came,
Yet, there was something in his eye, That won my love I knew not why.

The poor way-faring man.

2 Once when my scanty meal was spread,
He enter'd, not a word he spake,
Just perishing for want of bread,
I gave him all, he bless'd and brake
And ate, but gave me part again,
Mine was an angel's portion then,
And while I fed with eager haste,
The crust was manna to my taste.

3 I spied him where a fountain burst
Clear from the rock, his strength was gone,
The heedless water mocked his thirst,
He heard it, saw it hurrying on.
I ran and raised the sufferer up;
Thrice from the stream he drained my cup,
Dipped, and returned it running o'er,
I drank, and never thirsted more.

4 'Twas night. The floods were out; it blew
A wintry hurricane aloof,
I heard his voice abroad, and flew
To bid him welcome to my roof.
I warmed, I clothed, I cheered my guest,
Laid him on mine own couch to rest
Then made the earth my bed, and seemed
In Eden's garden while I dreamed.

5 Stripped, wounded, beaten nigh to death,
I found him by the high-way side;
I roused his pulse, brought back his breath,
Revived his spirit, and supplied
Wine, oil, refreshment: he was healed,
I had myself a wound concealed,
But from that hour forgot the smart,
And peace bound up my broken heart.

6 In pris'n I saw him, next condemn'd
To meet a traitor's doom at morn;
The tide of lying tongues I stemm'd
And honored him 'mid shame and scorn.
My friendship's utmost zeal to try,
He asked if I for him would die.
The flesh was weak, my blood ran chill,
But the free spirit cried "I will!",

7 Then, in a moment, to my view
The stranger started from disguise;
The tokens in his hands I knew,—
My SAVIOR stood before my eyes!
He spake, and my poor name he named,— [asham d;
" Of me thou hast not been e
These deeds shall thy memorial be,
Fear not, thou didst it unto me."

True Wisdom

1 Happy the man that finds the grace,
The blessing of God's chosen race;
The wisdom coming from above,
The faith that sweetly works by love.
Happy beyond description, he
Who knows "the Savior died for me!"
The gift unspeakable obtains,
And heavenly understanding gains

2 Wisdom divine! who tells the price
Of wisdom's costly merchandize?
Wisdom to silver we prefer,
And gold is dross compar'd to her.
Her hands are fill'd with length of days,
True riches, and immortal praise;
Riches of Christ, on all bestow'd,
And honor that descends from God.

3 To purest joys she all invites,
Chaste, holy, spiritual delights;
Her ways are ways of pleasantness,
And all her flowery paths are peace.
Happy the man who wisdom gains
Thrice happy who his guest retains:
He owns, and shall forever own,
Wisdom, and Christ, and heaven are one.

The Friend above all others.

Arranged and Harmonized for this work.

NOTE.—*The words to this tune are very much used by the Welch in times of revivals.*

There's a friend a-bove all oth-ers, Oh how he loves!

His is love be-yond a brother's, Oh how he loves!

Earthly friends may fail and leave us, This day kind, the next be-reave us;

But this friend will ne'er de-ceive us. Oh how he loves!

2 Blessed Jesus! would'st thou know him,
Oh, how he loves!
Give thyself e'en this day to him,
Oh, how he loves!
Is it sin that pains and grieves thee,
Unbelief and trials tease thee?
Jesus can from all release thee,
Oh, how he loves!

3 Love this friend who longs to save thee,
Oh, how he loves!
Dost thou love? He will not leave thee,
Oh, how he loves!
Think no more then of to-morrow,
Take his easy yoke and follow,
Jesus carries all thy sorrows,
Oh! how he loves!

4 All thy sins shall be forgiven,
Oh, how he loves!
Backward all thy foes be driven,
Oh, how he loves!
Best of blessings he'll provide thee,
Nought but good shall e'er betide thee,
Safe to glory he will guide thee,
Oh, how he loves!

5 Let us still this love be viewing,
Oh, how he loves!
And though faint keep on pursuing,
Oh, how he loves!
He will strengthen each endeavor,
And when pass'd o'er Jordan's river,
This shall be our song for ever,
Oh, how he loves!

Weep not for me.

1 When the spark of life is waning,
Weep not for me.
When the languid eye is stealing,
Weep not for me.
When the feeble pulse is ceasing,
Start not at its swift decreasing;
'Tis the fettered soul releasing,
Weep not for me.

2 When the pangs of death assail me,
Weep not for me.
Christ is mine, he cannot fail me,
Weep not for me.
Yes, though sin and doubt endeavor,
From his love my soul to sever,
Jesus is my strength for ever,
Weep not for me.

To-day the Savior calls. 6s & 4s.

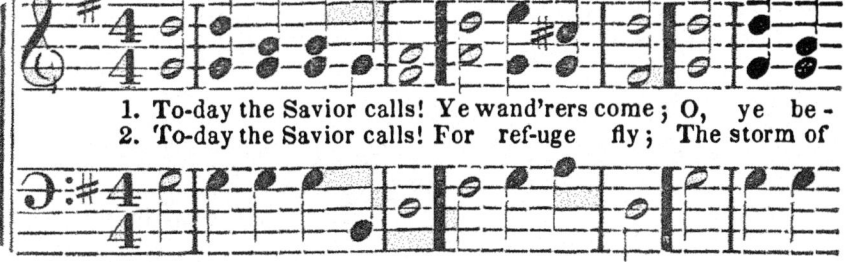

1. To-day the Savior calls! Ye wand'rers come; O, ye benighted souls, Why longer roam?
2. To-day the Savior calls! For refuge fly; The storm of vengeance falls; And death is nigh.

3
To-day the Savior calls!
Oh, hear him now:
Within these sacred walls
To Jesus bow.

4
The Spirit calls to-day!
Yield to his pow'r:
Oh, grieve him not away;
'Tis mercy's hour.

MY BELOVED. 8s & 7s.

1. This vain world, with all its pleasures, Very soon will be no more; There's no object worth admiring, There's no object worth admiring, But the God whom we adore.

2
See the happy spirits waiting,
  On the banks beyond the stream;
Sweet responses still repeating,
  Jesus, Jesus is their theme.

3
Hark! they whisper; lo! they call me,
  Sister spirit, come away;
Lo! I come; earth can't contain me,—
  Hail the realms of endless day.

4
Swiftly roll, ye lingering hours,
  Seraphs, lend your glittering wing;
Love absorbs my ransom'd powers,
  Heavenly sounds around me ring.

5
Worlds of light and crowns of glory,
  Far above yon azure sky!
Though by faith I now behold you,
  I'll enjoy you soon on high.

My Beloved.

1
My Beloved, wilt thou own me,
  When my heart is so defiled?
Though thy dying love has won me,
  Can I deem thee reconciled.

2
My Beloved, pass before me;
  Never from my sight remove.
Many waters, flowing o'er me,
  Cannot quench my burning love.

3
My Beloved, now endue me,
  With thine own attractive charms;
May thy spirit sweetly woo me;
  Fold me in thy sheltering arms.

4
My Beloved, kindly take me
  To thy sympathizing breast;
Never more will I forsake thee;
  Guide me to thine endless rest.

Mrs. Dana.

Hail! thou once despised Jesus. 8s & 7s. 91

1. Hail! thou once de-spis-ed Jesus, Hail thou
Thou didst suf-fer to re-deem us! Thou didst
By thy mer-its we find fa-vor; Life is
ev-er-last-ing King,
free sal-va-tion bring.
Hail thou ag-o-
gi-ven through thy name.
niz-ing Savior, Bearer of our sin and shame!

2 Jesus, hail! enthron'd in glory,
  There forever to abide!
All the heavenly hosts adore thee,
  Seated at thy Father's side;
There for sinners thou art pleading,
  There thou dost our place prepare;
Ever for us interceding,
  Till in glory we appear.

3 Worship, honor, power and blessing
  Thou art worthy to receive;
Loudest praises without ceasing,
  Meet it is for us to give;
Help, ye bright angelic spirits,
  Bring your sweetest, noblest lays;
Help to sing our Savior's merits;
  Help to chant Immanuel's praise.

THE PILGRIM'S FAREWELL.

1. Fare-well, fare-well, Farewell, dear friends, I must be gone, I have no home or stay with you; I'll take my staff and trav-el on, Till I a bet-ter world do view, I'll march to Canaan's land, I'll land on Ca-naan's

shore, Where pleasures never end, Where troubles come no more. Farewell, farewell, farewell, my loving friends, farewell.

2 Farewell, my friends, time rolls along,
Nor waits for mortal's care or bliss;
leave you here and travel on,
Till I arrive where Jesus is.
 I'll march, &c.

3 Farewell my friends, with many sighs,
And sorrow that no words can tell,
With bursting heart and weeping eyes,
I bid you all farewell, farewell.
 I'll march, &c.

4 Farewell, my brethren in the Lord,
To you I'm bound in cords of love ;
Yet we believe his gracious word,
That soon we all shall meet above.
 I'll march, &c.

5 Farewell, farewell ye saints of God,
Though many trials we have seen,
Yet we have loved the Savior's word,
And sweet our fellowship has been.
 I'll march, &c.

6 'Farewell, old soldiers of the cross,
You've struggled hard and long for heaven ;
You've counted all things here but loss,
Fight on, the crown will soon be given.'
 I'll march, &c.

7 Farewell, ye youth, be bold, be strong,
And firm the hallowed cross sustain ;
In Jesus' service, earthly loss,
Will but increase your heavenly gain.
 I'll march, &c.

8 Farewell, poor careless sinners, too,
It grieves my heart to leave you here,
Eternal vengeance waits for you ;
O turn, and find salvation near.
 I'll march, &c.

9 Farewell, my friends I soon shall rise,
And join the angelic host on high ;
I gaze on heaven with wishful eyes,
And long with angels' wings to fly.
 I'll march, &c.

94 — Awake, my soul. C. M. D.

Arranged and Harmonized for this work.

1. My drowsy pow'rs, why sleep ye so? A - wake, my slug-gish soul! Noth - ing hath half thy work to do, Yet nothing's half so dull. Go to the ants; for one poor grain, See how they toil and strive; Yet we who have a

heav'u t' ob-tain, How neg-li-gent we live.

2 We, for whose sake all nature stands,
And stars their courses move;
We, for whose guard the angel bands
Come flying from above.
We, for whom God the Son came down,
And labor'd for our good,
How careless to secure that crown
He purchased with his blood.

3 Lord, shall we live so sluggish still,
And never act our parts?
Come, holy Dove, from the heav'nly hill,
And warm our frozen hearts.
Give us with active warmth to move,
With vig'rous souls to rise;
With hands of faith and wings of love,
To fly and take the prize.

The Returning Wanderer.

1 O for a closer walk with God,
A calm and heavenly frame;
A light to shine upon the road
That leads me to the Lamb.
Where is the blessedness I knew,
When first I saw the Lord?
Where is the soul-refreshing view
Of Jesus and his word?

2 What peaceful hours I once enjoy'd,
How sweet their memory still!
But they have left an aching void
The world can never fill.
Return, O holy Dove, return,
Sweet messenger of rest!
I hate the sins that made thee mourn,
And drove thee from my breast.

3 The dearest idol I have known,
Whate'er that idol be,
Help me to tear it from thy throne,
And worship only thee.
So shall my walk be close with God,
Calm and serene my frame;
So purer light shall mark the road
That leads me to the Lamb.

Jesus' Love.

1 Plunged in a gulf of dark despair,
We wretched sinners lay,
Without one cheering beam of hope,
Or spark of glimm'ring day.
With pitying eyes the Prince of grace
Beheld our helpless grief;
He saw, and (O amazing love!)
He ran to our relief.

2 O for this love let rocks and hills
Their lasting silence break;
And all harmonious human tongues
The Savior's praises speak.
Angels, assist our mighty joys;
Strike all your harps of gold;
But when you raise your highest notes,
His love can ne'er be told.

The Key of Heaven.

1 Pray'r is the soul's sincere desire,
Unutter'd or express'd,
The motion of a hidden fire,
That trembles in the breast.
Pray'r is the burden of a sigh,
The falling of a tear,
The upward glancing of an eye,
When none but God is near.

2 Pray'r is the simplest form of speech,
That infant lips can try,
Pray'r the sublimest strains that reach
The Majesty on high.
Pray'r is the Christian's vital breath,
The Christian's native air;
His watch-word at the gate of death;
He enters heaven with prayer.

3 No prayer is made on earth alone,
The holy Spirit pleads,
And Jesus on the eternal throne
For sinners intercedes.
Oh, thou by whom we come to God,
The Life, the Truth, the Way;
The path of prayer thyself hast trod,
Lord, teach us how to pray.

96. The Voice of Mercy.

Arranged for this work.—Words by Rev. S. Hoyt.

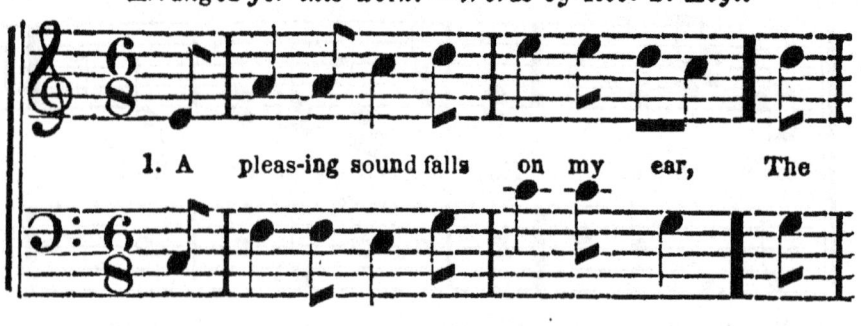

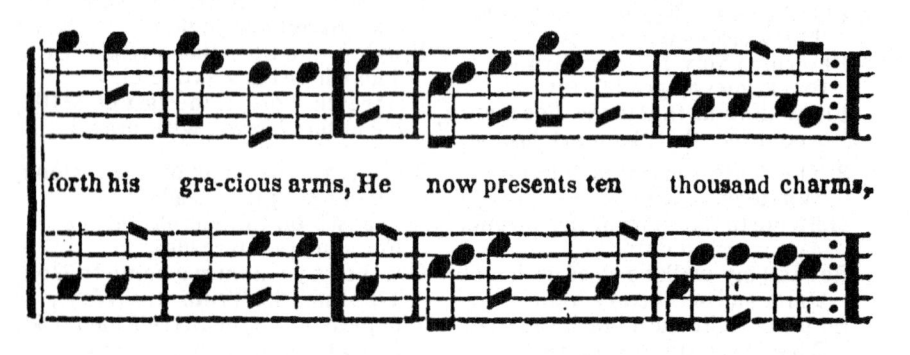

1. A pleas-ing sound falls on my ear, The voice of mer-cy do I hear? Oh, yes, for Je-sus Christ is near, To bless the weeping mourn-er; He stretch-es forth his gra-cious arms, He now presents ten thousand charms,

Be not dismay'd tho' fear a-larms, For Je-sus will re-ceive you.

Fine.

2 In melting accents hear him cry,
Come now to me, why will ye die?
O make one effort now, and try
To break the chain that binds you.
I'll take your load of guilt away,
And write your name above to-day,
And if you always watch and pray,
I never will forsake you.

3 I am both merciful and true,
And came to save just such as you;
For this the pains of death went through,
And thus procured your pardon.
And will you now my grace abuse?
My pardoning mercy still refuse?
O will you stay away and choose,
The road to death and sorrow?

4 Nay; Lord, I will, I do believe,
Thou wilt my guilty soul receive,
And from my load of guilt relieve,
And justify me freely.
I will no more in gloom repine,
For I am his, and He is mine;
His blessed light doth in me shine,
Dispersing all my darkness.

5 I'm happy now, my heart is free;
How could he save a wretch like me!
O, may my tongue forever be
Employed to spread his glory!
Let angels help me while I sing,
And all the saints their tribute bring;
Let Heaven and earth with praises ring,
Forever and forever.

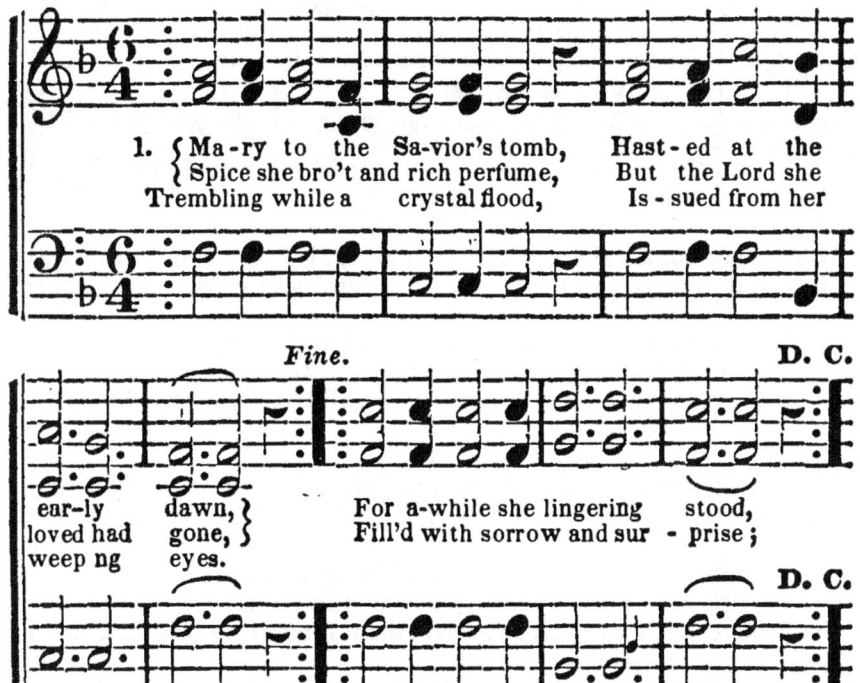

RESURRECTION. 7s. 8 lines.

1. Ma-ry to the Sa-vior's tomb, Hast-ed at the ear-ly dawn,
   Spice she bro't and rich perfume, But the Lord she loved had gone,
   Trembling while a crystal flood, Is-sued from her weeping eyes.
   For a-while she lingering stood,
   Fill'd with sorrow and sur-prise;

2 But her sorrows quickly fled
When she heard His welcome voice;
Christ had risen from the dead—
Now he bids her heart rejoice.
What a change his word can make,
Turning darkness into day;
Ye who weep for Jesus' sake,
He will wipe your tears away.

3 He who came to comfort her,
When she thought her all was lost,
Will for your relief appear
Though you now are tempest tost.
On His arm your burden cast;
On His love your thoughts employ;
Weeping for a while may last,
But the morning brings the joy.

98. Here is no rest.

Harmonized for this work. — Words by Rev. C. W. Ainsworth.

1. Here o'er the earth as a stranger I roam, Here is no rest,
Here as a pil-grim I wander alone, Yet I am blest,
My heart doth leap while I hear Jesus say, There, there is rest,
is no rest, For I look forward to that glo-ri-ous day,
I am blest. When sin and sor-row will van-ish a-way.
there is rest.

2
Here fierce temptations beset me around; Here is no rest—is no rest:
Here I am grieved while my foes me surround; Yet I am blest—I am blest.
    Let them revile me and scoff at my name,
    Laugh at my weeping—endeavor to shame;
I will go forward, for this is my theme; There, there is rest—there is rest.

3
Here are afflictions and trials severe; Here is no rest—is no rest;
Here I must part with the friends I hold dear; Yet I am blest—I am blest.
    Sweet is the promise I read in his word;
    Blessed are they who have died in the Lord;
They have been called to receive their reward;—There, there is rest—there is rest.

4
This world of cares is a wilderness state, Here is no rest—is no rest;
Here I must bear from the world all its hate,—Yet I am blest—I am blest.
    Soon shall I be from the wicked released,
    Soon shall the weary forever be blest,   [rest
Soon shall I lean upon Jesus' breast—There, there is rest—there is

My Love is Crucified. L. M. 6 lines.

Harmonized for this work.

1. O love divine, what hast thou done! Th'immortal God hath died for me, Th'immortal God for me hath died, My Lord, my love is crucified.

The Father's co-eternal son, Bore all my sins upon the tree! O sinner then thy Savior see, Remember him who died for thee.

2 Behold him, all ye that pass by,
  The bleeding Prince of life and peace!
Come see, ye worms, your Maker die,
  And say, was ever grief like his?
Come, feel with me his blood apply'd;
My Lord, my Love, is crucified.
  O, sinner then, &c.

3 Is crucified for me and you,
  To bring us rebels back to God;
Believe, believe the record true,
  Ye are all bought with Jesus' blood;
Pardon for all flows from his side;
My Lord, my Love, is crucified.
  O, sinner then, &c.

4 Then let us sit beneath his cross,
  And gladly catch the healing stream;
All things for him account but loss,
  And give up all our hearts to him;
Of nothing think or speak beside,
  My Lord, my Love, is crucified.
    O, sinner then, &c

THE GREAT PHYSICIAN. 7 & 6.

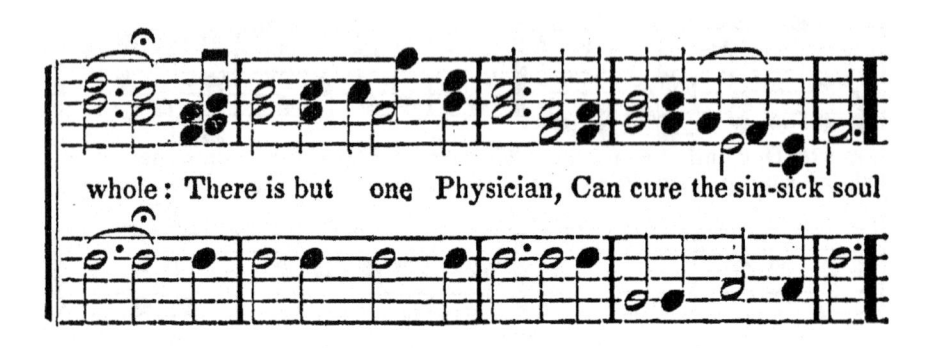

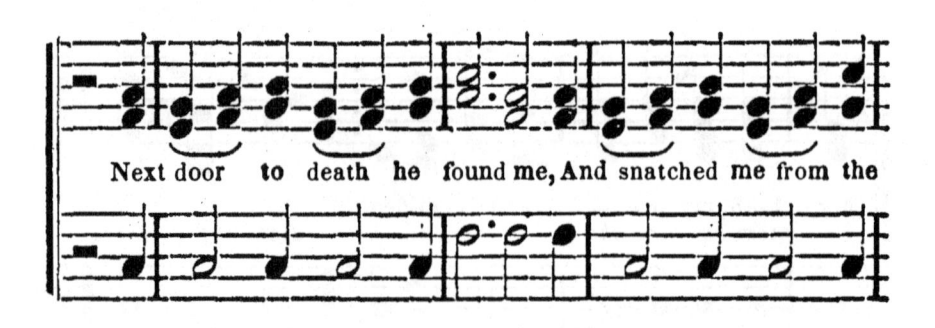

1. How lost was my condition, Till Jesus made me whole: There is but one Physician, Can cure the sin-sick soul Next door to death he found me, And snatched me from the grave, To tell to all around me, His wondrous power to save.

2
The worst of all diseases
 Is light, compared with sin;
On every part it seizes,
 But rages most within:
'Tis palsy, plague, and fever,
 And madness, all combined;
And none but a believer,
 The least relief can find.

3
From men great skill professing,
 I sought a cure to gain;
But this proved more distressing,
 And added to my pain.
Some said that nothing ailed me,
Some gave me up for lost,
Thus every refuge failed me,
And all my hopes were crossed

4
At length this great Physician,
 (How matchless is his grace)
Accepted my petition,
 And undertook my case:
First gave me sight to view him,
 For sin my eyes had sealed;
Then bade me look unto him,
 I look'd—and I was healed.

5
A dying, risen Jesus,
 Seen by an eye of faith,
At once from danger frees us,
 And saves the soul from death;
Come, then to this Physician,
 His help he'll freely give;
He makes no hard condition—
 'Tis only look and live.

SINNER COME. S. M.   L. MASON.

1. The Spirit in our hearts, Is whisp'ring 'Sinner, come;'
The bride, the church of Christ, proclaims, To all her children Come!'

2. Let him that heareth say To all about him, 'Come!'
Let him that thirsts for righteousness, To Christ, the fountain, come!'

3 Yes, whosoever will,
Oh let him freely come,
And freely drink the stream of life;
'Tis Jesus bids him come.

4 Lo! Jesus, who invites,
Declares, "I quickly come:"
Lord, even so! we wait thy hour;
O blest Redeemer, come!

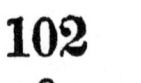

FREE GRACE. L. M.

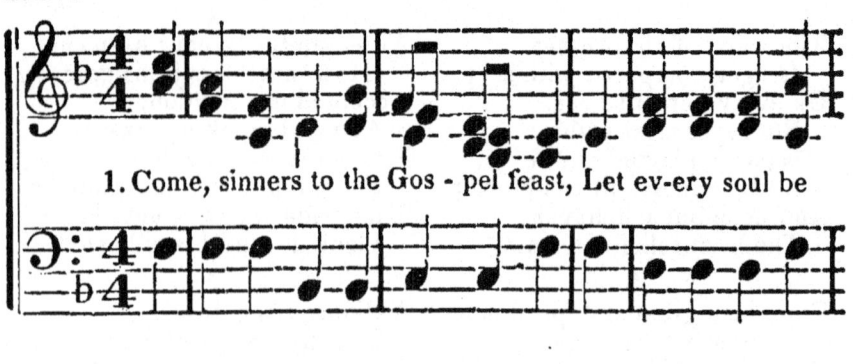

1. Come, sinners to the Gospel feast, Let every soul be Jesus' guest; Ye need not one be left behind, For God hath bidden all mankind. *Through grace, free grace, through grace, free grace, To ev-'ry child of Adam's race.*

The Gospel Feast.

2 Sent by my Lord, on you I call:
The invitation is to all;
Come, all the world! come, sinner [thou!
All things in Christ are ready now.
Through grace, &c.

3 Come, all ye souls by sin op-
press'd,
Ye restless wand'rers after rest;
Ye poor, and maim'd, and halt,
and blind,
In Christ a hearty welcome find.
Through grace, &c.

4 My message as from God re-
ceive;
Ye all may come to Christ and live;
O let his love your hearts constrain,
Nor suffer him to die in vain.
Through grace, &c.

5 See him set forth before your
eyes,
That precious, bleeding sacrifice!
His offer'd benefits embrace,
And freely now be sav'd by grace!
Through grace, &c.

I want to live a Christian here.

1. O that I had some humble place, Where I might hide from sorrow;
Where I might see my Savior's face, And there be freed from terror.

2. O had I wings like Noah's dove, I'd leave this world and Satan;
And fly away to realms above, Where Jesus stands inviting.

3 My heart is often made to mourn,
Because I'm faint and feeble;
And when my Savior seems to
frown,
My soul is filled with trouble;

4 But when he doth again return,
And I repent my folly,
'Tis then I after glory run,
And still the Savior follow

5 I want to live a Christian here,
I want to die while shouting :
I want to feel my Savior near,
When soul and body's parting.

6 I want to see bright angels
stand,
And waiting to receive me,
To bear my soul to Canaan's land,
Where Christ has gone before me.

JESUS IS REIGNING.

Arranged and Harmonized for this work.

1. Hail the day so long pre-dic-ted; Hark! the her-ald an-gels sing, Christ is born the much ex-pect-ed, Glo-ry to the new born King; Glory in the high-est, glo-ry, Peace on earth, good will to men; Je-sus, we her-ald, we

WESLEYAN PSALMIST.   105

her-ald, we her-ald, Je-sus we her-ald in Beth-le-hem.

2 Hark, again, the rocks are rending,
Earth unto her centre quakes;
Lo, the son of God is dying!
Satan's kingdom now he shakes.
Hear him crying, "It is finished,
I have paid the price for them."
Jesus is dying, &c.
Jesus is dying for sinful men.

3 Tune your harps, ye heavenly seraphs;
Shout ye followers of the Lamb;
Lo, he bursts the tomb and rises;
Jesus is the conqueror's name.
Angels now proclaim the tidings,
Hear him while he intercedes.
Jesus has risen, &c.   (*pleads.*
Jesus has risen; for sinners

4 See the eternal judge descending,
Seated on his Father's throne;
Thousand thousand hosts attending,
Swell the triumph of his train,
While the angel Gabriel sounding,
Earth and hell attend the call;
Jesus is coming, &c.
Jesus is coming, the Judge of all.

5 Now the judgment day is over;
Hell its prey has all received;
Heaven's heirs are crowned forever,
Such as have in Christ believed.
Angel and archangel vying,
Saints and seraphs join the cry.
Jesus is reigning, &c.   (*high.*
Jesus is reigning, the Lord most

Why Sleep Ye.   *Tune next Page.*

1 Why sleep ye, my brethren? come, let us arise,
O, why should we slumber in sight of the prize?
Salvation is nearer, our days are far spent,
O, let us be active; awake! and repent.
  Awake then ye slumb'rer, hear Jesus invite,
  Awake thou that sleepest, and I will give light.

2 O, how can we slumber! the Master is come,
And calling on sinners to seek them a home;
The Spirit and Bride now in concert unite,
The weary they welcome, the careless invite.
  Awake then, &c.

3 O, how can we slumber! our foes are awake;
To ruin poor souls every effort they make;
To accomplish their object no means are untried,
The careless they comfort, the wakeful misguide.
  Awake then, &c.

4 O, how can we slumber! when so much was done,
To purchase salvation by Jesus the Son!
Now mercy is proffer'd, and justice display'd,
Now God can be honor'd, and sinners be saved.
  Awake then, &c.

106. My soul's full of Glory. 11s.

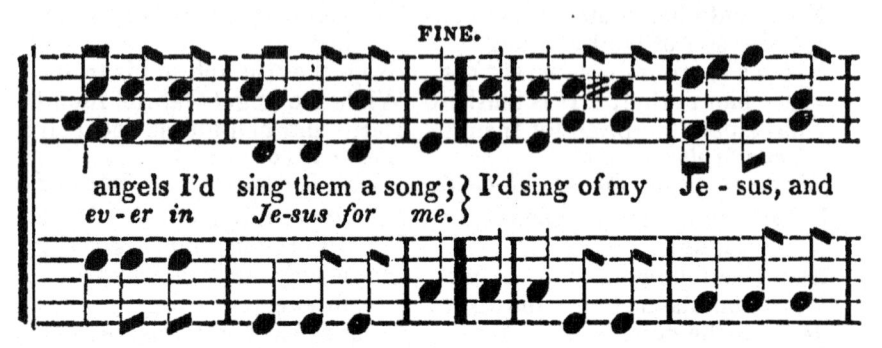

1 My soul's full of glory, Inspiring my tongue,
Could I meet with angels I'd sing them a song;
I'd sing of my Jesus, and tell of his charms,
And beg them to bear me to his loving arms.
  For glory, all glory in Jesus I see,
  It's glory forever in Jesus for me.

2 O Jesus! O Jesus! thou balm of my soul,
'Twas thou, my dear Jesus, that made my heart whole;
O, bring me to view thee, thou glorious King,
In oceans of glory thy praises to sing.
  For glory, &c.

3 A glimpse of bright glory surprises my soul,
I sing in sweet visions to view the bright goal;
My soul, while I'm singing, is leaping to go,
This moment for heaven, I'd leave all below.
  For glory, &c.

4 To the regions of glory my spirit shall flee,
And take this poor body immortal and free;
With angelic armies forever to blaze,
On Jesus's beauties forever to gaze.
  For glory, &c.

INDEX OF TUNES.

	PAGE		PAGE
Advent	16	Northfield	81
Awake my soul	94	O that will be joyful	4
Bright Canaan	15	O for that tenderness of heart	48
Behold I bring good tidings	33	O fly mourning sinner	58
Come to Jesus	9	O for a closer walk with God	78
Coronation	6	O land of rest	83
Canaan	38	Paradise	25
Come let us anew	57	Remember me	3
Come ye sinners	75	Rapture of love	41
Disciple	28	Resurrection	97
Expostulation	24	Shouting victory	34
Eden of Love	72	Sonnet	50
Fear not little flock	59	Saw ye my Savior	64
Free Salvation	66	Sinner can you hate the Savior	77
Fidelity	67	Star of Bethlehem	68
Free Grace	102	Sinner Come	101
God is love	20	The prodigal's return	8
Glory	26	The bleeding Savior	7
Give me Jesus	53	The Saint's home	30
Gethsemane	80	The Christian's triumph	35
Hail thou once despised Jesus	91	There are angels hovering round	39
Here is no rest	98	The pensive dove	43
I want to wear the crown	79	The good Shepherd	74
I want to live a Christian	103	The pearl of great price	76
Jerusalem	12	The beloved of Zion	84
Jesus Reigns	32	The poor wayfaring man	86
Jesus says he will be with us	70	The friend above all others	88
Jesus is reigning	104	To day the Savior calls	89
Love Divine	60	The voice of mercy	96
Lo I am with you	36	The glorious treasure	52
Langtree	44	The judgment scene	56
Longing for Christ	46	The Lord will provide	71
Lenox	62	The pilgrim's farewell	92
Lovest thou me	85	The great Physician	100
Laban	51	Woodland	10
Millennial Dawn	22	Wesleyan Chapel	18
My Beloved	90	Will you go	40
My love is crucified	99	When we all meet in heaven	65
My soul's full of glory	106	What glorious tidings	82

INDEX OF FIRST LINES.

Alas and did my	3..7	A pleasing sound falls on my ear	96
All hail the great	6	Be it my only wisdom	19
Afflictions though they seem	8	Blow ye the trumpet	63
Arise my soul to Pisgah's	13	Come on my partners in	18
And am I only	19	Come thou fount of every	26
Away with our sorrow	49	Children of the Heavenly	35
Arise, my soul arise	62	Come let us anew	57
A poor wayfaring man	86	Come sinners to the	69..102

INDEX.

	PAGE.		PAGE.
Children of God renounce	70	O glorious hope of	19
Come ye sinners poor and	75	O how happy are they	41
Come and let us sweetly	55	O tell me where the dove	43
Delay not—delay not	59	O joyful sound of	45
Earth rejoice our Lord	32	O for that tenderness	48
From Heaven's blissful regions	23	O 'tis delight without	49
Farewell dear friends	92	O fly mourning sinner	58
Glory to God I have	59	O for a closer walk	95..78
Glory, honor, power	27	O land of rest for thee	83
How lost was my	23..100	O thou in whose presence	84
How happy every child	13	O no we cannot sing	79
Hark! what mean	27	O thou who driest the	79
Hail the blest morn	33	O love divine what hast	99
How happy is the Pilgrim's	38	O that I had some humble	103
How tedious and tasteless	46	Plunged in a gulf of dark	95
Ho, every one that thirsts	69	Prayer is the soul's sincere	95
Hark my soul it is	85	Religion is a glorious	52
Happy the man that	87	Sweet the moments	29
How sweet to reflect	72	Saw ye my Savior	64
Here o'er the earth as	98	Sweet is the work my God	69
Hail the day so long	104	Since man by sin has	83
I want a principle	11	There is an hour of	10
I have started for	31	This world is all a fleeting	11
I would not live alway	37	This world's not all a fleeting	11
Jerusalem my happy	12..44	There is a land of pure	15
Jesus I my cross have	28	The morning light is	22
Jesus my all to Heaven	79	The Lord into his garden	25
Lift up your hearts to	13	The Lord is our Shepherd	36
Lo! on a narrow neck	19	Thou sweet gliding Kedron	37
Love divine all love	27..60	Thou Shepherd of Israel	47
Let earth and Heaven	63	The wondrous love of Jesus	65
Let thy kingdom blessed	74	The Pearl that worldlings	76
Lord we come before thee	55	There's a friend above	88
Let every mortal ear	81	This vain world with all	90
Mid scenes of confusion	30	To-day the Savior calls	89
My God, I know, I feel	45	The judgment day is	56
My span of life will	45	Tho' troubles assail	71
Man at his first creation	66	The Spirit in our hearts	101
My beloved wilt thou	90	When I can read my	4..34
My soul be on thy guard	51	What sound is this salutes	16
My drowsy powers why	94	What sound is this? A Song	20
Mary at the Savior's tomb	97	What's this that steals	21
Now the Savior stands	77	We're travelling home	40
O turn ye! O turn ye	24	What now is my object	47
O when shall I see Jesus	23	When all thy mercies	49
O could I speak the	17	When for eternal worlds	50
O love divine how sweet	17	While I'm happy hear me	53
Our souls by love	49..5	What glorious tidings	82
On Jordan's stormy	7	When marshalled on the	68
O for a thousand tongues	7	Ye who know your sins	61
O for a heart to praise	11	Ye ransomed sinners	63